ISBN   979-8-9922481-1-1

Other Scriptures noted

The Amplified Version (AMP)

King James Version (KJV)

New American Standard Version (NASB)

New International Version (NIV)

This book is dedicated to the Glory of God and to Jesus Christ His Son. It was the vision God gave for the book that prompted its beginnings. It was the constant encouragement of the Holy Spirit that kept me working at this book when time constraints seemed impossible to make it happen.

Furthermore, I would like to thank and honor my friends: Bishop Randy Morgan, Apostle Mike Whited and Dan Hall, and Apostle Shelly Planellas, who saw the need for this book. This book kept getting prophesied at the Immersed Conference in Atlanta for two years in a row. Also, my sisters Brenda and Stacy who encouraged and supported me all along the way. Last but not least, I want to thank my loving spouse, Jerry Wright, and our church New Life Community Gospel whose constant love, prayers, support, and encouragement made this possible. You're remarkable!

Rev. Samuel Kader

Contents

Introduction

Isaiah 43:19

Behold, I will do a **new thing**, Now it shall spring forth; Shall you not
know it? I will even make a road in the wilderness *And* rivers in the
desert.

Throughout History God has been doing a new thing. The Old Testament reveals individuals called by God, such as Abraham. His tribe
grew into a nation. Eventually they were held captive as slaves in Egypt
and God sent a deliverer, Moses, to lead His people out of slavery and
into the promised land. But as we will see, Moses was challenged by
the people of God over and over again. This nation of Hebrews were
referred to, biblically, as the Church in the Wilderness.

Once they settled into the Promised land with the Covenant of the
law, the prophets promised a coming Messiah. But when Jesus arrived,
the Moses followers, God's people, refused to hear Him and had Him,
their deliverer, crucified.

Then as the ancient Roman Empire declared Christianity to be the
state religion, and under penalty of death, pagans were forced to declare their allegiance to the state religion. This infusion of unbelievers

into the Church watered down the influence of the Holy Spirit and the Church world plunged into the Dark Ages.

Near the end of the Dark Ages, as the Renaissance began blossoming, God began restoring His Church to the truth that had been lost. He did this as a process over the centuries. This restoration to the glory and power of the first century church happened, and is happening, as God raised up individuals to lead the church back to its intended purpose. But at every turn, the former move rejected and still rejects the new thing God is trying to restore.

Thus, we will look at how the Church has fought God, and how it is still fighting God. As Jesus said to Paul on the road to Damascus:

Acts 9; 3-5 (Ampified) 3 Now as he (Paul) traveled on, he came near to Damascus, and suddenly a light from heaven flashed around him,4 And he fell to the ground. Then he heard a voice saying to him, Saul, Saul, why are you persecuting Me [harassing, troubling, and molesting Me]? 5 And Saul said, Who are You, Lord? And He said, I am Jesus, Whom you are persecuting. *It is dangerous and it will turn out badly for you to keep kicking against the goad [to offer vain and perilous resistance].*

When the Church fights God, it is useless, it is dangerous, and it turns out badly. Perhaps we can learn from the history of the church and not make the same mistakes over and over again. This is my hope.

Thus, we begin in the time of Moses with the Church in the Wilderness and move forward from there.

Chapter One

When the Church Fights God

The Church in the Wilderness

Ancient Israel was called the Church in the Wilderness according to the book of Acts. Yet when ancient Israel, the people of God, were in the wilderness, headed to the promised land and out of Egyptian slavery, they simply would not follow God's instructions. Moses was God's appointed leader who personally heard from God, and yet nonetheless they rebelled again and again.

Acts 7:38-39

"This is he (Moses) who was in the congregation[1] (ie Church) in the wilderness with the Angel who spoke to him on Mount Sinai, and *with* our fathers, the one who received the living oracles to give to us, [39] whom our fathers would not obey, but rejected.

This assembly of God's people, thus referred to as the Church in The Wilderness, had a God appointed leader, Moses. God personally called Moses to lead His people into the promised land. Initially, Moses was a reluctant leader. But God gave him signs and miracles to show to Moses as well as His people that Moses was His anointed leader. These signs were to reveal that God had a plan and a purpose to bring them out of bondage and into the Promised Land.

As they started out on their journey, the people fought God's plan, they walked in fear rather than faith and murmured and complained during the entire journey. When they found themselves in the desert and cried out for water, God gave them a miracle and provided water out of a rock. But God's miracles were never enough to build faith in them.

Exodus 17:1-6

Then all the congregation of the children of Israel set out on their journey from the Wilderness of Sin, according to the commandment of the Lord, and camped in Rephidim; but *there was* no water for the people to drink. [2] Therefore the people contended with Moses, and said, "Give us water, that we may drink." So Moses said to them, "Why do you contend with me? Why do you tempt the Lord?" [3] And the people thirsted there for water, and the people complained against Moses, and said, "Why *is* it you have brought us up out of Egypt, to kill us and our children and our livestock

---

1. Gr. *ekklesia, assembly* or *church*

with thirst?" [4] So Moses cried out to the Lord, saying, "What shall I do with this people? They are almost ready to stone me!" [5] And the Lord said to Moses, "Go on before the people, and take with you some of the elders of Israel. Also take in your hand your rod with which you struck the river, and go. [6] Behold, I will stand before you there on the rock in Horeb; and you shall strike the rock, and water will come out of it, that the people may drink." And Moses did so in the sight of the elders of Israel.

When they became hungry, God had a supernatural plan to feed them. [2]

According to **Exodus 16** and **Numbers 11**, God's plan was to provide Manna from Heaven; actual Angels' food.

Psalm 78:23-25

Yet He had commanded the clouds above, And opened the doors of heaven,[24] Had rained down manna on them to eat and given them of the bread of heaven.[25] Men ate angels' food; He sent them food to the full.

In **Numbers 11:5-6** the people argued with God's provision, complained about this "miserable manna" They instead wanted some meat. The NIV version in verse 6 says "But now we have lost our appetite; we never see anything but this manna!"

Accordingly, God provided the meat as they demanded, but it made them sick.

Moses heard from God face to face and gave the people the directions that God provided. But still they wanted to fight God's plans.

Some of the worst rebellions against God's chosen leadership came from Moses' own relatives. His brother and sister, Aaron and Miriam,

---

2. Exodus 16; 1-35, Numbers 11:1-9

started to complain about Moses' Ethiopian wife. [3] From there they started to consider why was Moses even the leader? Weren't they his siblings and just as good and anointed as him? They said, "Has the Lord indeed spoken only through Moses? Has He not spoken through us also?[4] God got angry with their proud assumptions and caused Miriam to break out in leprosy. Fighting God is bad for your health!

But they weren't the only family members who fought God's choice of leadership.

Numbers 16: 1-3

Korah, son of Izhar, the son of Kohath, the son of Levi, and certain
    Reubenites—Dathan and Abiram, sons of Eliab, and On son of
    Peleth, became insolent [2] and rose up against Moses. With them
    were 250 Israelite men, well-known community leaders who had
    been appointed members of the council. [3] They came as a group
    to oppose Moses and Aaron and said to them, "You have gone too
    far! The whole community is holy, every one of them, and the Lord
    is with them. Why then do you set yourselves above the Lord's
    assembly?

Korah was a first cousin to Moses, as their fathers were brothers.
So, as such, he felt he was just as holy and anointed as his cousin, and
didn't see why he shouldn't lead the people as well. God didn't see it
that way and it came to a showdown.

Numbers 16 [31] Now it came to pass, as he (Moses) finished speaking
    all these words, that the ground split apart under them, [32] and
    the earth opened its mouth and swallowed them up, with their
    households and all the men with Korah, with all *their* goods. [33] So

---

3. Numbers 12: 1-16

4. Numbers 12:2 NKJV

they and all those with them went down alive into the pit; the earth closed over them, and they perished from among the assembly.

As Jesus said to Saul in **Acts 9:4-5** in the *Amplified Bible*

4 And he fell to the ground. Then he heard a voice saying to him, Saul, Saul, why are you persecuting Me [harassing, troubling, and molesting Me]?

5 And Saul said, Who are You, Lord? And He said, I am Jesus, Whom you are persecuting. *It is dangerous and it will turn out badly for you to keep kicking against the goad [to offer vain and perilous resistance].*

It is dangerous and it turns out badly for the Church to fight God, offering vain and perilous resistance.

> **It is dangerous and it turns out badly for the Church to fight God, offering vain and perilous resistance.**

As Hebrews chapter 3 points out, God was not pleased with all this murmuring, complaining and rebellion against His plans. In fact, a whole generation did not make it out of the desert.

Hebrews 3 :7-19

7 Therefore, as the Holy Spirit says: "Today, if you will hear His voice,

8 Do not harden your hearts as in the rebellion, In the day of trial in the wilderness, 9 Where your fathers tested Me, tried Me,

And saw My works forty years. 10 Therefore I was angry with that generation,

And said, 'They always go astray in their heart, And they have not known My ways.'

11 So I swore in My wrath, 'They shall not enter My rest.' "

12 Beware, brethren, lest there be in any of you an evil heart of unbelief in departing from the living God; 13 but exhort one another daily,

while it is called "Today," lest any of you be hardened through the deceitfulness of sin. 14 For we have become partakers of Christ if we hold the beginning of our confidence steadfast to the end, 15 while it is said:

"Today, if you will hear His voice, do not harden your hearts as in the rebellion."

16 For who, having heard, rebelled? Indeed, was it not all who came out of Egypt, led by Moses? 17 Now with whom was He angry forty years? Was it not with those who sinned, whose corpses fell in the wilderness? 18 And to whom did He swear that they would not enter His rest, but to those who did not obey? 19 So we see that they could not enter in because of unbelief.

So, from the beginning, God's people, the church, fought God. and for those who did, it did not turn out well for them. The exceptions were Joshua and Caleb who actually obeyed and followed God wherever He led.

Chapter Two

Why The Church Fights God

Ephesians chapter six lets us know that we do not actually fight people (flesh and blood) but we do fight against the demonic realms.

Ephesians 6:10-13

[10] Finally, my brethren, be strong in the Lord and in the power of His might. [11] Put on the whole armor of God, that you may be able to stand against the wiles of the devil. **[12] For we do not wrestle against flesh and blood, but against principalities, against powers, against the rulers of the darkness of this age, against spiritual *hosts* of wickedness in the heavenly *places*.** [13] Therefore take up the whole armor of God, that you may be able to withstand in the evil day, and having done all, to stand.

God's enemy, Satan, knows the principle in **Matthew 12** that a house divided will not stand. So, he attempts to keep the church at war with itself and against the plans and purposes of God.

Matthew 12:25-28

[25] But Jesus knew their thoughts and said to them: "**Every kingdom divided against itself is brought to desolation, and every city or house divided against itself will not stand**. [26] If Satan casts out Satan, he is divided against himself. How then will his kingdom stand? [27] And if I cast out demons by Beelzebub, by whom do your sons cast *them* out? Therefore they shall be your judges. [28] But if I cast out demons by the Spirit of God, surely the kingdom of God has come upon you.

So, although people are fighting the current move of God, we find that throughout history the enemy who is behind this action, Satan, attempts to thwart God's plans with each new and current move. Typically, we find the tools Satan uses are fear, a resistance to change, and a desire to keep or regain the power that the former move provided to certain individuals. We can expect to see these actions repeated throughout history as God keeps moving His Church forward. So, it is not a surprise when we see the Church fighting God.

Fighting Moses (the Church in the Wilderness)

According to **Acts 7:38** God's movement to get the children or Israel out of slavery in Egypt was noted as the *Church in the Wilderness*. So from this point forward we begin to see the people of God fighting God in every new move He births.

Miriam and Aaron

According to **Numbers 12:1-9** Moses' siblings, Miriam and Aaron begin to rebel against their brother. God clearly intervenes and tells them that He is the one who called Moses into the leadership of this church in the wilderness.

Numbers 12:1-9 states:

Then Miriam and Aaron spoke against Moses because of the Ethiopian woman whom he had married; for he had married an Ethiopian woman. [2] So they said, "**Has the Lord indeed spoken only through Moses? Has He not spoken through us also?**" And the Lord heard *it.* [3] (Now the man Moses *was* very humble, more than all men who *were* on the face of the earth.)

[4] Suddenly the Lord said to Moses, Aaron, and Miriam, "Come out, you three, to the tabernacle of meeting!" So the three came out. [5] Then the Lord came down in the pillar of cloud and stood *in* the door of the tabernacle, and called Aaron and Miriam. And they both went forward. [6] Then He said,

"Hear now My **words: If there is a prophet among you, I, the Lord, make Myself known to him in a vision; I speak to him in a dream.** [7] **Not so with My servant Moses; He *is* faithful in all My house.** [8] **I speak with him face to face, even plainly, and not in dark sayings; And he sees the form of the** Lord. Why then were you not afraid to speak against My servant Moses?"

[9] So the anger of the Lord was aroused against them, and He departed.

[10] And when the cloud departed from above the tabernacle, suddenly Miriam *became* leprous, as *white as* snow.

Though this was their brother, they became critical of his choices, firstly because he married someone outside of Israel. Then with this critical spirit, they attempted to assume the leadership position he had. They began to say that they were anointed just as much as Moses, so why shouldn't they also rule. God stepped in and clearly laid out that not only was Moses His choice of leadership, but that Moses and God had a special relationship unlike any other. God spoke to Moses face to face. Aaron and Miriam were aware of this yet were not afraid to speak against God's anointed choice. The church in the wilderness tried to fight God. This attempt to fight God failed miserably.

Even despite this lesson, Aaron operated out of fear and made a golden calf shaped idol, out of the church's earrings. For this God would have killed Aaron but did not, only because Moses interceded in prayer. (Exodus 32)

Exodus 32:2-6

And Aaron said to them, "Break off the golden earrings which *are* in the ears of your wives, your sons, and your daughters, and bring *them* to me." **3** So all the people broke off the golden earrings which *were* in their ears and brought *them* to Aaron. **4** And he received *the gold* from their hand, and he fashioned it with an engraving tool, and made a molded calf.

Then they said, "This *is* your god, O Israel, that brought you out of the land of Egypt!"

5 So when Aaron saw *it,* he built an altar before it. And Aaron made a proclamation and said, "Tomorrow *is* a feast to the Lord." **6** Then they rose early on the next day, offered burnt offerings, and brought peace offerings; and the people sat down to eat and drink, and rose up to play.

The entire Congregation

Since their mission was to enter and occupy the promised land of Israel, Moses sent twelve spies into Israel to scope out the land. Of course, two, Joshua and Caleb, saw the promised land through eyes of faith. The other ten saw it as an impossible task and spoke from a place of fear. Their fear was contagious and caused the church in the wilderness to reject God's plan for them. They wanted to turn back to slavery in Egypt regardless of what God said.

Numbers 14: 1-10

So all the congregation lifted up their voices and cried, and the people wept that night. **2** And all the children of Israel complained against Moses and Aaron, and the whole congregation said to them, "If only we had died in the land of Egypt! Or if only we had died in this wilderness! **3** Why has the Lord brought us to this land to fall by the sword, that our wives and children should become victims? Would it not be better for us to return to Egypt?" **4** So they said to one another, "Let us select a leader and return to Egypt."

5 Then Moses and Aaron fell on their faces before all the assembly of the congregation of the children of Israel.

6 But Joshua the son of Nun and Caleb the son of Jephunneh, *who were* among those who had spied out the land, tore their clothes; **7** and they spoke to all the congregation of the children of Israel, saying: "The land we passed through to spy out *is* an exceedingly good land. **8** If the Lord delights in us, then He will bring us into this land and give it to us, 'a land which flows with milk and honey.' **9** Only do not rebel against the Lord, nor fear the people of the land, for they *are* our bread; their protection has departed from them, and the Lord *is* with us. Do not fear them."

10 And all the congregation said to stone them with stones. Now the glory of the Lord appeared in the tabernacle of meeting before all the children of Israel.

Again, as the church in the wilderness fought God, it did not turn out well for this rebellion. Those who rebelled were now doomed to wander in that wilderness for another forty years until they all died off.

***

Korah, his cousin

In Numbers 16, we see Korah, Moses' cousin rising up against God's
chosen leader.

Numbers 16:1-3

Now Korah the son of Izhar, the son of Kohath, the son of Levi,
with Dathan and Abiram the sons of Eliab, and On the son of Peleth,
sons of Reuben, took *men;* **2** and **they rose up before Moses with
some of the children of Israel, two hundred and fifty leaders
of the congregation,** representatives of the congregation, men of
renown. **3** They gathered together against Moses and Aaron, and said
to them, "*You take* **too much upon yourselves, for all the congregation** *is* **holy, every one of them,** and the Lord *is* among them.
**Why then do you exalt yourselves above the assembly of the
Lord?**"

Even though they had seen what happened to Miriam when she and
her brother Aaron rose up against Moses, now their cousin decided he
should be in charge.

Numbers 12:28-35

28 And Moses said: "By this you shall know that the Lord has sent
me to do all these works, for *I have* not *done them* of my own will.
29 If these men die naturally like all men, or if they are visited by the
common fate of all men, *then* the Lord has not sent me. **30** But if the
Lord creates a new thing, and the earth opens its mouth and swallows

them up with all that belongs to them, and they go down alive into the pit, then you will understand that these men have rejected the Lord."

31 Now it came to pass, as he finished speaking all these words, that the ground split apart under them, **32** and the earth opened its mouth and swallowed them up, with their households and all the men with Korah, with all *their* goods. **33** So they and all those with them went down alive into the pit; the earth closed over them, and they perished from among the assembly. **34** Then all Israel who *were* around them fled at their cry, for they said, "Lest the earth swallow us up *also!*"

35 And a fire came out from the Lord and consumed the two hundred and fifty men who were offering illegal incense before God.

Again, God fought those who were opposing Him and His plan. The church was fighting God, but it did not work out well for Korah or his comrades. Instead, God fought for Moses and God's plan moved forward.

With every move of God, a point person is chosen to be the catalyst and give birth to the Divine plan. But rebellious human nature often opposes the one chosen by God. Satan inspires this division, in order to fight God. We see that with Moses' followers. Yet Scripture makes it clear that God has an order to His Kingdom, and God always wins.

Hebrews 13: 17 says it this way:

Hebrews 13:17

17 Obey those who rule over you, and be submissive, for they watch out for your souls, as those who must give account. Let them do so with joy and not with grief, for that would be unprofitable for you.

It certainly turned out unprofitable for Miriam, Aaron, and their cousin Korah.

***

Fighting Jesus

Throughout the Gospels we find the religious leaders fighting Jesus at every turn. People tend to get comfortable with their tradition and keep God in a box of their making. To the first century Jews, who were the former move of God, nothing more was needed than obeying Moses and the laws. The Apostle Paul realized that no one can actually keep the Hebrew laws, and consequently through those laws, none are righteous.

Romans 3:10-19

[10] As it is written: "**There is none righteous, no, not one;**[11] There is none who understands; There is none who seeks after God.[12] They have all turned aside; they have together become unprofitable; There is none who does good, no, not one."[13] "Their throat *is* an open tomb; With their tongues they have practiced deceit"; "The poison of asps *is* under their lips";[14] "Whose mouth *is* full of cursing and bitterness."[15] "Their feet *are* swift to shed blood;[16] Destruction and misery *are* in their ways;[17] And the way of peace they have not known."[18] "There is no fear of God before their eyes." [19] Now we know that whatever the law says, it says to those who are under the law, that every mouth may be stopped, and all the world may become guilty before God.

So, in and of ourselves, we cannot become righteous in the sight of God, and not by our keeping the laws of Moses. It is by faith that we're saved. Yet in the first century the former move of God decided to persecute the present move of God (Jesus, the Messiah Savior). They felt that they had all they needed and had no interest in this particular Savior.

In Acts 7 Stephen points out to the Jews, the former move of God, that though they thought Moses and the law were all that was needed, they never kept it anyway.

Acts 7:51-53

51 "*You* stiff-necked and uncircumcised in heart and ears! You always resist the Holy Spirit; as your fathers *did,* so *do* you. 52 Which of the prophets did your fathers not persecute? And they killed those who foretold the coming of the Just One, of whom you now have become the betrayers and murderers, 53 who have received the law by the direction of angels and have not kept *it.*"

The former move of God, (the Moses' followers) killed Stephen for saying so. Even as Jesus demonstrated the love of God in action, they rejected the message of salvation. Jesus healed the sick, cast out demons, raised the dead, yet they rejected Him. The church (the former move of God, the church in the wilderness) fought God once again.

This new move of God over-ruled the requirement of the laws of Moses by replacing it with faith in the son of God.

John 3:5-8, 16

5 Jesus answered, "Most assuredly, I say to you, unless one is born of water and the Spirit, he cannot enter the kingdom of God. 6 That which is born of the flesh is flesh, and that which is born of the Spirit is spirit. 7 Do not marvel that I said to you, 'You must be born again.' 8 The wind blows where it wishes, and you hear the sound of it, but cannot tell where it comes from and where it goes. So is everyone who is born of the Spirit."

16 For God so loved the world that He gave His only begotten Son, **that whoever believes in Him should not perish but have everlasting life**. 17 For God did not send His Son into the world

to condemn the world, but that the world through Him might be saved.

18 "**He who believes in Him is not condemned**; but he who does not believe is condemned already, because he has not believed in the name of the only begotten Son of God. **19** And this is the condemnation, that the light has come into the world, and men loved darkness rather than light, because their deeds were evil. **20** For everyone practicing evil hates the light and does not come to the light, lest his deeds should be exposed.

Faith in Jesus was a whole lot easier than keeping all the laws of Moses, which no one could actually do. Yet they rejected this free gift of salvation.

They kept God in their religious box and anything that upset their rule and order they assumed must be from the demonic realm.

Matthew 12:22-24

22 Then one was brought to Jesus one who was demon-possessed, blind and mute; and He healed him, so that the blind and mute man both spoke and saw. **23** And all the multitudes were amazed and said, "Could this be the Son of David?"

24 Now when the Pharisees heard *it* they said, "**This *fellow* does not cast out demons except by Beelzebub, the ruler of the demons**."

Likewise in John 9, a man born blind was healed by Jesus, and yet these religious leaders, the Pharisees, were the blind ones, unable to see this was the hand of God, doing a new thing in their midst.

John 9:13-16

13 They brought him who formerly was blind to the Pharisees. **14** Now it was a Sabbath when Jesus made the clay and opened his eyes. **15** Then the Pharisees also asked him again how he had received his sight. He said to them, "He put clay on my eyes, and I washed, and I see."

¹⁶ Therefore some of the Pharisees said, "This Man is not from God, because He does not keep the Sabbath."

Keeping their religious ceremonies was more important than seeing God work a miracle in their midst. In the end, they chose to fight God and have Jesus put to death. The former move of God fought the current move of God. However, they never expected God to outwit their conniving scheme and raise Christ from the dead. This resurrection ended the need for the laws of Moses, since now God had defeated sin, death and the grave. Eternal life and righteousness were all now imputed to those who believed in Christ as the Savior of the world.

> In the end, they chose to fight God and have Jesus put to death.

Romans 10:8-13

⁸ But what does it say? "The word is near you, in your mouth and in your heart" (that is, the word of faith which we preach): ⁹ that **if you confess with your mouth the Lord Jesus and believe in your heart that God has raised Him from the dead, you will be saved**. ¹⁰ For with the heart one believes unto righteousness, and with the mouth confession is made unto salvation. ¹¹ For the Scripture says, **"Whoever believes on Him will not be put to shame."** ¹² For there is no distinction between Jew and Greek, for the same Lord over all is rich to all who call upon Him. ¹³ For "**whoever calls on the name of the Lord shall be saved.**"

Moses played his part, but God moved far beyond keeping the law. He crucified it and opened a marvelous and miraculous gateway into eternal life through faith in Jesus Christ.

Chapter Three

EPHESIANS 6
Warfare in the
House

The Real Battle

S omething significant to know is, though we feel like we are fighting and arguing with people, there is a bigger picture. Ephesians 6 tells us to put on the full armor of God because we are not warring against people, but against spiritual, unseen, but very real entities from the demonic world. These entities fight God and God's purposes continuously. Though they already lost the war at the Cross of Calvary, until the Lord returns, they fight nonetheless. And their main target is the people of God. So, as Judas Iscariot betrayed Jesus when Satan entered him, so emissaries from Hell inspire people to make bad choices fighting God's purposes, without realizing it. They are sure they are in the right, and are standing up for God, when in fact they are fighting Him.

2 Corinthians 2 [10] Now whom you forgive anything, I also *forgive.* For if indeed I have forgiven anything, I have forgiven that one for your sakes in the presence of Christ, [11] *lest Satan should take advantage of us; for we are not ignorant of his devices.*

2 Corinthians 11 [12] But what I do, I will also continue to do, that I may cut off the opportunity from those who desire an opportunity to be regarded just as we are in the things of which they boast. [13] For such *are false apostles, deceitful workers, transforming themselves into apostles of Christ.* [14] *And no wonder! For Satan himself transforms himself into an angel of light.* [15] *Therefore it is no great thing if his ministers also transform themselves into ministers of righteousness,* whose end will be according to their works.

Satan is subtle. He disguises himself and his workers as if they are indeed righteous, holy, and working for God. Thus, Korah, Moses' cousin, sounded reasonable when he refused to obey God's appointed leadership. But he was dangerously wrong. It was his undoing as he fought against God, not merely Moses.

***

Jesus and the Pharisees

The former move of God had been Moses and the Law. Then here comes a current move of God and the former move immediately rejects what God is doing. Jesus comes as the Savior of the world, and the very Messiah that Moses and the prophets proclaimed would come, but the religious righteous, the proud Pharisees, rejected and even fought against God.

They were certain they were right, and that the traditions they had handed down from their ancestors were the last and final move of God. Oh, sure, someday a Messiah would come, but only to vindicate them against the Roman Empire, and their other enemies. They were certain that they were the chosen.

John 7: 1-5

After these things Jesus walked in Galilee; for He did not want to walk in Judea, because *the Jews sought to kill Him*. [2] Now the Jews' Feast of Tabernacles was at hand. [3] His brothers therefore said to Him, "Depart from here and go into Judea, that Your disciples also may see the works that You are doing. [4] For no one does anything in secret while he himself seeks to be known openly. If You do these things, show Yourself to the world." [5] *For even His brothers did not believe in Him*.

Mathew 9:16-17

[16] No one puts a piece of unshrunk cloth on an old garment; for the patch pulls away from the garment, and the tear is made worse. [17] **Nor do they put new wine into old wineskins,** or else **the wineskins break, the wine is spilled, and the wineskins are ruined**. But they put new wine into new wineskins, and both are preserved."

This is the reason the former move always fights the new move of God. It can't contain it. The old former move is like old wineskin and cannot hold the new thing God is doing because they won't make room for it. They are too rigid and stuck in their old ways. New wineskins are required to contain a fresh wind of the Spirit.

In particular, the Pharisees fought and even hated Jesus because He broke their rigid rules about the Sabbath.

They were responsible for bringing Him to Rome's governor, Pilot, to silence this unsettling challenge to their religion.

God's people, the Jews, sought to kill Jesus. Just as Moses' brother and sister, as well as his cousin Korah, challenged Moses. Additionally, the brothers of Jesus challenged Him. They simply did not believe what God was doing, and thought they knew better.

Jesus was the new move of God. He showed the love and mercy and compassion of God. He healed the sick, He raised the dead, He fed the multitudes. He did so many miracles they could not all be counted.

John chapter 21: 25 says

And there are also many other things that Jesus did, which if they were written one by one, I suppose that even the world itself could not contain the books that would be written. Amen.

Nonetheless, the Pharisees did everything they could to fight and destroy God's new move in the Earth. They arrested Jesus and got Pilot to crucify Him.

Once Jesus was raised from the dead, He ascended to Heaven and sent the Holy Spirit to infill His church. As He promised in **Acts 1:8,** once they were filled with the Holy Spirit, they would have power to preach this good news of the resurrection wherever God sent them – to Jerusalem, Samaria, and the uttermost parts of the earth. The former move would have none of that!

They thought crucifying Jesus was the end of the challenge to their religious status quo. Now here come the apostles and disciples of Jesus preaching with the anointing of the Holy Spirit, right in the Jewish Temple. The Pharisees decided they needed to kill this move off quickly. They arrested God's point persons and brought them before the Council. In **Acts 5** we see one wise man, Gamaliel, understands how dangerous it is to fight against God.

Acts 5:26-42 [26] Then the captain went with the officers and brought them without violence, for they feared the people, lest they should be stoned. [27] And when they had brought them, they set *them* before the council. And the high priest asked them, [28] saying, "Did we not strictly command you not to teach in this name? And look, you have filled Jerusalem with your doctrine, and intend to bring this Man's blood on us!" [29] But Peter and the *other* apostles answered and said: "**We ought to obey God rather than men. [30] The God of our fathers raised up Jesus whom you murdered by hanging on a tree. [31] Him God has exalted to His right hand** *to be* Prince and Savior, **to give repentance to Israel and forgiveness of sins. [32] And we are His witnesses to these things**, and *so* also *is* the Holy Spirit whom God has given to those who obey Him." [33] When they heard *this,* they were furious and plotted to kill them. [34] **Then one in the council stood up, a Pharisee named Gamaliel, a teacher of the law held in respect by all the people, and commanded them to put the apostles outside for a little while.** [35] And he said to them: "**Men of Israel, take heed to yourselves what you intend to do regarding these men.** [36] For some time ago Theudas rose up, claiming to be somebody. A number of men, about four hundred, joined him. He was slain, and all who obeyed him were scattered and came to nothing. [37] After this man, Judas of Galilee rose up in the days of the census, and drew away many people after him. He also perished, and all who obeyed him were dispersed. [38] **And now I say to you, keep away from these men and let them alone; for if this plan or this work is of men, it will come to nothing; [39] but if it is of God, you cannot overthrow it—*lest you even be found to fight against God.*"** [40]

And they agreed with him, and when they had called for the apostles and beaten them, they commanded that they should not speak in the name of Jesus and let them go. So, they departed from the presence of the council, rejoicing that they were counted worthy to suffer shame for His name. And daily in the temple, and in every house, they did not cease teaching and preaching Jesus *as* the Christ. Because Gamaliel recognized this new move, these Christ followers, could actually be of God, they were not killed, not at this time. But this did not stop the former move of God from persecuting the current move of God. It did not stop God, either.

Once Jesus was raised from the dead and the day of Pentecost had come, the new move of God, the Christian Church arose in power. Then a new adversary arose as well.

***

Saul of Tarsus

Feeling that he had to fight for God and God's honor, as well as the honor of Moses, Saul of Tarsus set out to destroy this new move of God. He was certain that these Jesus followers were heretics defiling the good name of God's people. He took it on himself to eradicate this Christian threat.

Of course, as the former move of God attempts to resist God, and fight what God is doing in the Earth, it turns out badly. However, in Saul's case, Jesus stopped him in his tracks as he was on his way to Damascus to arrest any Christians he might find. Saul was blinded, was converted to Christ, and became a prolific warrior for the Gospel. He was transformed from Saul of Tarsus, the sworn enemy of the Church, to Paul the Apostle, the great defender of the faith.

(Saul) Acts 9:1-19

Acts 8:3

[3] As for Saul, he made havoc of the church, entering every house, and dragging off men and women, committing *them* to prison.

Acts 9:1-4

Then Saul, still breathing threats and murder against the disciples of the Lord, went to the high priest [2] and asked letters from him to the synagogues of Damascus, so that if he found any who were of the Way, whether men or women, he might bring them bound to Jerusalem.

[3] As he journeyed, he came near Damascus, and suddenly a light shone around him from heaven. [4] Then he fell to the ground, and heard a voice saying to him, "Saul, Saul, why are you persecuting Me?"

[5] And he said, "Who are You, Lord?"

Then the Lord said, "I am Jesus, whom you are persecuting. It *is* hard for you to kick against the goads."

The Amplified version[1] translated **Acts 9:3-5** this way:

[3] Now as he traveled on, he came near to Damascus, and suddenly a light from heaven flashed around him,

---

1. https://www.biblegateway.com/versions/Amplified-Bible-Classic-Edition-AMPC/ (AMPC)Copyright © 1954, 1958, 1962, 1964, 1965, 1987 by http://www.lockman.org/

⁴ And he fell to the ground. Then he heard a voice saying to him, Saul, Saul, **why are you persecuting Me** [harassing, troubling, and molesting Me]?

⁵ And Saul said, Who are You, Lord? And **He said, I am Jesus, Whom you are persecuting.** *It is dangerous and it will turn out badly for you to keep kicking against the goad [to offer vain and perilous resistance].*

Once Paul was converted to Christ, He became just as zealous for Christ as he had been against Him.

The Apostle Paul then began to see that God had opened the doors of the Gospel to not only Jewish people but the gentile world as well. This was too much for the Pharisees, Moses' followers. If God wanted to admit gentiles into His Kingdom, then they *had to convert* to Judaism. They assumed, you can't do a *new* thing; instead, you have to *become one of us* if you want to serve God correctly.

They invaded one of the early primarily gentile churches in Antioch and insisted that these new gentile believers become circumcised and follow the laws of Moses. This resulted in a council held in Jerusalem to study the matter. The issue, the Pharisees contended, was that Jesus was not enough. You had to add Moses to Jesus to be politically correct.

Acts 15:1-2 "And certain men came down from Judea (to Antioch) and taught the brethren, "Unless you are circumcised according to the custom of Moses, you cannot be saved.""

Paul and Barnabas disputed this, that no one needs to add Moses onto Jesus, but faith in Christ alone is enough. The dispute could not be settled in that local church in Antioch, so a conclave was held at the mother church in Jerusalem to settle the matter.

Acts 15:6-11 **⁶** Now the apostles and elders came together to consider this matter. **⁷** And when there had been much dispute, Peter rose up *and* said to them: "Men *and* brethren, you know that a good while ago God chose among us, that by my mouth the Gentiles should hear the word of the gospel and believe. **⁸** So God, who knows the heart, acknowledged them by giving them the Holy Spirit, just as *He did* to us, **⁹** and made no distinction between us and them, purifying their hearts by faith. **¹⁰** Now therefore, why do you test God by putting a yoke on the neck of the disciples which neither our fathers nor we were able to bear? **¹¹** But we believe that through the grace of the Lord Jesus Christ we shall be saved in the same manner as they."

It was determined that faith in Christ was enough. Additionally, they gave these new gentile believers some additional practical advice. There was no intention of burdening them with Moses and the law.

Acts 15:28-29

²⁸ For it seemed good to the Holy Spirit, and to us, to lay upon you no greater burden than these necessary things: **²⁹** that you abstain from things offered to idols, from blood, from things strangled, and from sexual immorality. If you keep yourselves from these, you will do well.

Jesus was raised from the dead and God's new move, the Christian Church, was birthed on the day of Pentecost. As for the Church in the Wilderness, Jerusalem was ultimately attacked by Rome. The Jewish Temple was destroyed, the Mosaic Priesthood was obliterated, and the Church of the Wilderness, the people of Moses, went into exile. **Fighting God did not turn out well**.

Christ Jesus, the Savior of the world was victorious, and God's new thing flourished even through Roman persecution. The devil wasn't done with attacks, however. So, he had the world infiltrate the church. The Roman Emperor, Constantine, in 313 A.D. in the Edict of Milan, decriminalized Christianity and ceased persecution. In the **Edict of**

Thessalonica in 380 A.D. Christianity was declared to be the official religion of the Roman empire. Refusal to become Christian meant certain death. Thus, pagans took oaths to say they were Christians and infiltrated the Church while still holding their pagan beliefs and rituals. This watered down the gospel by becoming a mixture of truth and superstition. By 400 AD the Church was merely an empty shell. The rite of baptism was considered unimportant, many put it off until their death bed, *if at all*. Baptism was considered of no real significance.[2]

After 400 A.D., the Christian Church had two main components, The Eastern Church located in Constantinople, whose Bishop oversaw the churches in that region, and the Western Church located in Rome, whose Bishop oversaw the rest of the known world.

Many points of disagreement cropped up, but the differences in the languages spoken and the customs of the people of the East and the West were not trivial.[3]

The Muslim conquest of Syria, Palestine, and Egypt removed the patriarchs of Antioch, Jerusalem and Alexandria as rivals to the Bishop of Rome. Those grave disasters brought increasing power and authority to the head of the church in Rome. In 1054 A.D. the eastern and western parts of the church formally separated. The Patriarch of Constantinople was supreme in the East, and the Patriarch of Rome was supreme in the West. Pope Leo of Rome sent a letter to the Patriarch of Constantinople, which was laid on the high altar of St. Sophia's

---

2. Iverson, Dick, *Present Day Truths*, ABC Publishing, 2008, .pg 40

3. Kuiper, B.K., The Church in History, WM.B. Eerdmans Publishing Co, Grand Rapids MI, 1955.Page 119

church, formally excommunicating the Patriarch, Cerularius. In like fashion Pope Leo was sent a letter from the East excommunicating him. The separation was complete.

Over the next centuries, the church of Rome, with the kings of Europe under his control, became more and more corrupt and power hungry. At that time, the people were mostly uneducated and relied on their priest to explain the things of God. Bibles were not written in the common language, and the laity had no access to the truth of God's word.

This was the setup for God's next move.

Chapter Four

Fighting the Early Christians

Fighting Luther

On February 27, 380 AD, Roman Emperor Theodosius I made Christianity the state religion of the empire with the publishing of the Edict of Thessalonica. It had become a favored religion by Emperor Constantine earlier in that century.[1]

As such pagan religions were no longer in favor.

---

1. "The Edict of Thessalonica | History Today". www.historyto-day.com. *Retrieved 09-13-2023.*

In 392 Emperor Theodosius outlawed heathen worship under penalty of death. The church that had begun by being persecuted was now the persecutor of the heathen. This was nothing like Christ,

To gain favor in the Empire, pagans began to flood Christian churches, declaring they were also Christians without any true conversion, and bringing their pagan ways with them. This began diluting Christianity, to the point that it became a system of rules and works. Baptism lost any meaning to a church that was mostly heathen.[2]

Because the Empire had given tax exemption to the clergy, yet unwilling to lose tax revenue, clergy status was given to the poorest and least educated populace. Thus *the Jeroboam system* was in place.[3]

1 Kings 12: 28-33

[28] Therefore the king asked advice, made two calves of gold, and said to the people, "It is too much for you to go up to Jerusalem. Here are your gods, O Israel, which brought you up from the land of Egypt!" [29] And he set up one in Bethel, and the other he put in Dan. [30] Now this thing became a sin, for the people went *to worship* before the one as far as Dan. [31] He made shrines on the high places, **and made priests from every class of people, who were not of the sons of Levi.**

[32] Jeroboam ordained a feast on the fifteenth day of the eighth month, like the feast that was in Judah, and offered sacrifices on the altar. So he did at Bethel, sacrificing to the calves that he had made. And **at Bethel he installed the priests of the high places which he**

---

2. Iverson, Dick; *Present Day Truths*, Mannah House Resource, Portland OR, 1976 pg. 39

3. Ibid pg. 40

had made. [33] So he made offerings on the altar which he had made at Bethel

The church of the Middle Ages became a false religious system taking the name of Christ. People who no longer followed the Holy Spirit did not trust a God they did not know, so they trusted their Bishops. People who did not know God did not know how to pray, so they needed liturgies to follow.[4]

It's easy to see how a church that had rules, and trusted their unsaved leaders, got further from the light of the Gospels. Rome, which had once been the head of the Roman Empire easily became the seat of the new religious system. The Great Schism of 1054 A.D. caused the separation of the Roman Catholic Church from the Eastern Orthodox Churches after the mutual excommunication of one another. The primary causes of the Schism were disputes over papal authority—the Pope claimed he held authority over all of Christianity including the Eastern Greek-speaking patriarchs.

Ultimately the Pope, seen as the Vicar of Christ, had full authority over all Catholic churches and lands. Jesus was not consulted, the Holy Spirit was not consulted, the Pope was the one declaring doctrine for believers. Truly the Dark Ages had arrived.

Thus, the religious system, the Church that existed in the 1500s was dark, devoid of life and relegated to the rules of Rome. Martin Luther appeared on the scene as a young Monk desperately wanting to get right with God. The traditions of the Church, and Indulgences in particular, which were paid to the church in order to release souls from eternal damnation, was disconcerting to Luther. He fasted, he made pilgrimages to Rome, he tried everything that he was taught in

---

4. Ibid pg 41

order to right his soul with God. Yet he still felt guilty and miserable. But in 1517 as he cried out to God, God met him. **Romans 1:16-17** suddenly hit him, and he received the revelation that the just *shall live by faith*, not works.

Luther found his freedom in the Good News of the Gospel and was certain that his superiors and the Church would rejoice in this profound truth. They did not.

God opened a door. A new revelation unfolded as God restored to His church the truth which had been lost for centuries. But the former move of God, the fallen unredeemed Catholic Church immediately labeled Luther a heretic. A price was placed on his head.

The church was again fighting God.

Because it was God Who was moving and the Holy Spirit was once again hovering over the face of the deep, many people chose to follow Luther despite the danger. A fire had been ignited, a fresh move of God was birthed. It could not be stopped. This new move of God restored light to God's people. This movement was named after God's point person, and its followers became known as Lutherans. Thus, the Lutheran Church was born.

> A fire had been ignited, a fresh move of God was birthed. It could not be stopped

This did not, however, dissolve the highly organized system of works. The Roman Church tried to stop these "heretics" at every opportunity.

Chapter Five

The Reformation

John Wycliffe and John Huss

John Wycliffe was born in England in 1320. He studied at Oxford University and became a professor there.

During his early life the Black Death of the Middle Ages had ravished Europe. By 1353 when it finally ended, Wycliffe had lost many of his friends. By that time half of the population of England had died. As a scholar, he received his formal education at the University of Oxford. He therefore had access to the Latin Bible, and it was there he found solace. He began calling for reform of the Catholic Church and declared that the Bible, not the Church should be the rule of faith. Since most Bibles in use were written in Latin as translated from Hebrew and Greek by Jerome, Wycliffe began translating the Bible into English making it accessible to the general population.

Wycliffe's call for the purity of the church to be restored, and for false doctrines to be rejected, infuriated the Catholic clergy, bishops and even the pope. Thus, in 1377 the pope wrote an official bull (papal demand) to the University of Oxford. In it he demanded that the University pluck up Wycliffe and his doctrines by the root to dispose of them.

He wrote in the harshest language in the bull that "one John Wycliffe, professor of divinity, has gone to such a pitch of detestable folly, that he fears not to teach, and publicly preach, or rather to vomit out of the filthy dungeon of his breast, certain erroneous and false propositions and conclusions, savoring even of heretical (de)pravity, tending to weaken and overthrow the status of the whole Church... and some of Christ's flock he hath been defiling therewith, and misleading from the straight path of the sincere faith into the pit of perdition."[1]

Though the Bishop of Canterbury along with other bishops were determined to carry out the Pope's decree, they were prevented by England's nobility. Also in the same year, this same Pope Gregory XL died.

After the pope's death, a schism arose between powerful political potential popes from Rome and those of France. This schism lasted 39 years until the Council of Constance in 1417 A.D.

Besides translating the Bible into English, Wycliffe also wrote many other books. Though he was a hunted man by the Church, yet pow-

---

1. 2 Foxe, John, _Foxe's Book of Martyrs_, Whitaker House, Springdale PA 15144, 1981. pages 58-59.

erful English nobles protected him, and he died in peace on December 31, 1384. [2]

After his death, his teachings still went forward. His followers, known as Lollards, denounced the pope, practiced poverty and accepted the Bible as the source of theological truth.

In Bohemia, John Huss (also known as Jan Hus or Jon Hus) was among those influenced by Wycliffe. Huss fervently grabbed onto Wycliffe's teachings. Born around 1369, and trained for the priesthood, Huss became the Dean of Theology at the University of Prague. He condemned the selling of indulgences, though he had at one time supported this practice of buying entrance into Heaven for departed loved ones or for yourself.

Pope John XXIII excommunicated John Huss, but Huss declared it to be null and void. To bring about peace, end schisms, and bring about reforms in the church, Emperor Sigismund called for a council in 1414. Huss arrived for the council on November 2, 1414 with the promise of safety from the Emperor.

Nonetheless, the Church had him arrested as a heretic. Though the Emperor and his people protested his arrest, heretics had no rights and promises made to one need not be kept. Furthermore, it was considered an act of piety to betray a heretic. He was kept in prison until July 6th, 1415. He was then brought before the bishops and in the presence of his Emperor, he was dressed in priestly garments, then as one by one they were removed, curses were pronounced over him. He was then crowned with a paper cap with three devils painted on it declaring here is the heretic. Finally, John Huss was led to the stake and burned to death as a martyr.

---

2. Kuiper, B.K. Page 192

The same Council of Constance that burned Huss alive, then ordered that all of Wycliffe's writings should be burned and that Wycliffe's bones be exhumed and burned. It took until 1428 until the grave of Wycliffe was discovered and opened. With great ceremony the bones were burned and his memory cursed. His ashes were then tossed into the Severn River to be carried out to sea.

Nonetheless, Wycliffe's ministry was not destroyed. Bibles are printed and still being translated in the language of the people around the world. People can read the word of God for themselves in print, online, in and e-books. What the church deemed heresy was then the current move of God and it could not be stopped even by burning the books and the bodies of the authors.

As of September 2023, the Bible has been translated into 736 languages, with the New Testament translated into an additional 1,658 languages, and smaller portions of the Bible translated into 1,264 other languages. This means that at least some parts of the Bible have been translated into 3,658 languages. According to Ethnologue, there are 7,097 known languages in the world. At least one part of the Bible has been translated into 3,312 of the 7,097 languages.[3]

***

3.

https://www.christianlingua.com/into-how-many-languages-has-the-bible-been-translated/#:~:text=The%20complete%20Bible%20has%20been,3%2C312%20of%20the%207%2C097%20languages . Last accessed 9/12/2024

Martin Luther

In Florence Italy, a priest named Savonarola, preached against the excesses of luxury and the wickedness within the Catholic Church. He included Pope Alexander VI in his tirades against evil. Thus in 1498 he was hanged and his body burned. [4]

From 1445 to 1456 a professor in the University of Erfurt in Germany, **John of Wessel**, a leading scholar of his time, preached that we are justified by faith alone, he attacked indulgences, and other doctrines of the Catholic Church. Luther once said, "If I had read the works of Wessel beforehand, it might have seemed that I derived all my ideas from him." [5] Wessel was tried for heresy by the Archbishop of Mainz. He tried to defend himself, but failed. He then recanted but was thrown in prison where he died in October 1489.

Martin Luther was born on November 10, 1483. He was too young to have heard or been acquainted with the teachings of Wessel.

Since Luther had not previously read the works of Wessel, it was the Holy Spirit at work, revealing a truth to be restored; that salvation was by faith and not by works. Luther's voice rang across Germany and eventually through Europe as well. The Church of that day tried its best to silence Luther and his followers. But they could not fight God. This truth was restored.

Luther was ordained a priest in 1507, to his father's chagrin, since his father wanted Martin to be a lawyer. Doing his best to be an

---

4. Kuiper, B.K. Page 199

5. Ibid pg. 200

effective and loyal Catholic priest, Luther made a trip to Rome in 1511.

He tried to obtain his way into Heaven by works. As a monk in a monastery, he performed the humblest of tasks; sweeping the floors cleaning the cells of other monks, dusted, prayed, fasted. He wasted away until he looked like a skeleton.[6] He thought of Christ as an angry God, ready to throw souls in hell.

At the end of 1512, while meditating on Romans chapter one, the words of St. Paul pierced his soul. **"The just shall live by faith**." **(Romans 1:17)** opened his eyes, his heart and his soul to the truth God was restoring to the Church.

So, on **October 31, 1517 he nailed his ninety five thesis to the door of the Castle Church in Wittenberg**. Should the Church accept his thesis, their lucrative income from selling indulgences, as a means of personal forgiveness and the supposed release of deceased relatives from Purgatory would cease. The church took a stand to once again fight God and resist the Holy Spirit.

In 1520, they demanded that Luther renounce all of his writings. This he could not do. After a debate in July 1519 against a papist, Eck, he became convinced that the doctrines posed by John Huss, a century prior, were true.

Pope Leo excommunicated Luther in a bull on June 15, 1520 [7] which stated that all of Luther's books were to be burned, and Luther was forbidden to preach. He and his followers were given sixty days to recant, and if not, they were to be imprisoned. But Luther's followers

---

6. Ibid pg. 213

7. Kuiper Pg. 230

took the copies of the papal bull and threw them in the river. They could not be enforced.

Luther discovered that the printing press was effective in shaping public opinion. Thus, he gained supporters all over his beloved Germany and well beyond its borders.

Since Pope Leo's excommunication had little effect, Luther was called to an inquiry at the Diet of Worms in 1521. There Luther was condemned as an outlaw by Charles V.

Nonetheless as the conference ended, after several days of confusion Luther slipped away into hiding. It was the hope of the Pope that he had been murdered. Rumors to that effect circulated around Europe. But for ten months he was held as guest in the castle Warburg of Frederick the Wise.

When Luther died on 18 February 1546, Pope Leo X's excommunication was still considered in effect. None of this stopped the truth as the movement Luther started grew exponentially. Luther translated the Bible from Latin into German, making it accessible to the common people.

William Tyndale could not get his English translation of the Bible's New Testament printed in England, so he went to visit Martin Luther, and in 1525 had it published in the city of Worms. His translation was from the original Greek, not the Latin Vulgate as John Wycliffe had done before him.

But if the populace could read the Word for themselves, they would have a measuring stick of truth to compare against the fallacies their priests espoused.

The Word of God is alive and active and sharper than a two-edged sword. (**Hebrews 4:12**)

Eventually William Tyndale's enemies captured him and had him burned alive at the stake on October 6, 1536 near Brussels.

But the final truth that God brought forth through Luther was that it is by faith that we are saved, not by works. Though the Roman Church of Luther's day tried to fight him, they were fighting God, and God's truth could not be contained.

Chapter Six

Anabaptists

Once Luther had the revelation that salvation was by faith alone, and born again believers began to seek the Lord, additional revelation began to surface.

Balthasar Hubmaier (1480 – March 10, 1528); was an influential German Anabaptist leader. He was one of the most well-known and respected Anabaptist theologians of the Reformation.[1] What led him and others to this new revelation was built upon what Luther had taught.

They began to reason, if salvation came by faith, then how could an infant make such a profession of faith. Thus, they denounced the Catholic and Lutheran practice of infant baptism. Many believers understood this truth and began to be baptized as adult believers. They re-instituted the believer's baptism by immersion. This was a

---

1. https://en.wikipedia.org/wiki/Balthasar_Hubmaier last accessed November 21, 2024

restoration of truth from the early first century church that had been lost in the dark ages.

This group, now called Anabaptists were violently persecuted. The former move of God (Lutherans and Catholics) began to fight the new thing God was doing. Lutherans, though still persecuted by Catholics, now joined forces with them against the Anabaptists. In a devious pretense of offering these believers a baptism by immersion, they were instead held under water until they drowned.[2] . In some cases, they were placed in cages and lowered into a river and left to drown.

On March 10, 1528, Hubmaier was executed by burning in the public square. Three days later, after his execution, his wife had a stone tied around her neck and was drowned in the Danube River. Indeed, the church was fighting God. It seems whenever God restores a truth or expands our understanding of His truth, humans fight God. We are so certain that the revelation we have is the whole truth and nothing but the truth, so help us God. Yet God is not done bringing truth to His people.

Remember in John chapter 8, Jesus said the truth would set us free. However, there was a condition to obtaining this truth

John 8:31-32

31 Then Jesus said to those Jews who believed Him, **"If you abide in My word**, you are My disciples indeed. 32 And you shall know the truth, and the truth shall make you free."

"IF" is a condition we must meet.

IF we ABIDE in HIS WORD...

---

2. Iverson, Dick, *Present Day Truths*, ABC Book Publishing, May 1, 2008, page 75

The condition for knowing truth is to maintain an ongoing relationship with Jesus through His written word. Through this means, over time, more and more understanding unfolds. This is what has happened in history. People had a certain amount of truth, and from that foundation God gave revelation to build upon. Line upon line, precept upon precept, little by little. revealed truth is built upon (**Isaiah 28:10-13**). We cannot pretend to know all truth or to know all that God knows. As God declares in

Isaiah 55:8-9

8 "For My thoughts *are* not your thoughts, Nor *are* your ways My ways," says the Lord. 9 "For *as* the heavens are higher than the earth, So are My ways higher than your ways, And My thoughts than your thoughts.

and according to **Amos 3:7** Surely the Lord God does nothing unless He reveals His secret to His servants the prophets.

> Surely the Lord God does nothing, unless He reveals His secret to His servants the prophets.

God has a point person, one with whom He trusts to birth a new thing in the Earth. Thus, a Moses arises, a Martin Luther or someone with whom He can trust to bring forth the new current move of God. The responsibility is heavy, but the Holy Spirit drives them on. So, though Balthasar Hubmaier was executed, the truth moved forward. Today there are many churches which accept believer's baptism as the norm. But God wasn't done yet.

Chapter Seven

Pentecostals

After the movements of salvation by faith and believer's baptism were pretty much established, other truths were yet to be restored. Next was the Holiness movement. The Holiness movement traces back to John Wesley and his Methodist Church but kept expanding into other groups as well.

"In 1843 about two dozen ministers withdrew from the Methodist Episcopal Church to found the Wesleyan Methodist Church of America, establishing a pattern of defections or looser ties. Sizable numbers of Protestants from the rural areas of the Midwest and South were joining the Holiness movement. These people had a penchant for strict codes of dress and behavior. Most of them had little sympathy for the "superficial, false, and fashionable" Christians allegedly preoccupied with wealth and social standing"[1]

---

1. https://www.britannica.com/topic/Pentecostalism last accessed November 21, 2024

Many groups became part of the Holiness movement including the Nazarenes, Christian Missionary Alliance, Salvation Army, and the Church of God (Anderson, Indiana). As these church groups and individuals sought a second blessing or a deeper walk with God, they saw there was so much more in the Bible listed in the Book of Acts and about the first century early church.

As they got more determined to hear from God and to experience His presence all the more, a new truth was restored to the church. Pentecostalism began to explode at the turn of the 20th century. We now move forward to William Seymour and Charles Fox Parham.

William Seymour and Charles Fox Parham

The Early Pentecostals

Charles Fox Parham (June 4, 1873 – January 29, 1929) had pastored a Methodist Church prior to founding a Bible school in Topeka Kansas. He taught the essence of the Holiness doctrine. Over the Christmas holiday, he gave the students at his Bible school in Topeka, Kansas an assignment: to discover what was the initial Biblical physical evidence if a believer had been baptized with the Holy Spirit. The students concluded that speaking in tongues was the answer. One of his students, therefore, Agnes Ozman, told her Pastor, Rev. Parham, that she believed if he would lay hands on her that she would receive this baptism. Thus on January 1, 1901 Agnes began speaking in tongues, in her new Heavenly language. [2]

Within a few days, Parham himself and about half of his students were all so baptized.

Charles Fox Parham then began travelling the nation with this message of the baptism of the Holy Spirit with the evidence of speaking in tongues. In December 1905 Parham opened another Bible school in Houston Texas. One notable student was William Seymour. Due

---

2. Stanley M. Burgess & Gary B. McGee, *Dictionary of Pentecostal and Charismatic Movements*, Zondervan Publishing House, Grand Rapids, Michigan. 1988, page 660

to contracted smallpox, Seymour was a one-eyed 34-year-old. He was the son of former slaves and was an associate minister in a Houston church.

Because Seymour was black, he was not allowed to sit in the classroom with the other white students, but took a seat in the hallway where he could hear the teachings. Though Seymour did not receive the baptism of the Holy Spirit at that time, he was convinced of it. He moved to Los Angeles where Seymour eventually started a church. At first it was in a home, Seymour and his small group of new followers then soon relocated to the home of Richard and Ruth Asberry at 214 North Bonnie Brae Street. The crowds got so large that the front porch of this home collapsed. A new location was obtained at 312 Azusa Street in Los Angeles. This had been a barn and flies would often enter the building. But the Holy Spirit was there in great power. Not only did people receive the Holy Spirit baptism manifested by speaking in tongues, as well other gifts of the Spirit listed in 1 Corinthians 12, but also many miraculous healings took place.

Again, the church world wanted to mock and criticize what God was doing there, the press was cruel, yet more and more people from around the world came to the Azusa Street mission. Sometimes young men would stick their heads into the open windows to cat call and make fun. But the power of the Holy Spirit was so strong they'd come under conviction and run to the altar to get saved. More than once the fire brigade was called because onlookers were certain the building was on fire. It was the holy presence of God.

Yet the former move of God, particularly the Holiness churches began to call this the work of the devil and rejected what God was doing. Even so, during the height of the Jim Crow laws in America, whites and blacks worshipped together at the Azusa Street Mission. Seymour often said, "*The color line was washed away in the Blood*".[3]

But many denominations from the Holiness era would have nothing to do with any Pentecostal group. They warned their people to stay clear of those "Holy Rollers" as if they were demon possessed. Many began to form doctrines to state that the gifts of the Holy Spirit, especially speaking in tongues had died off in the first century when the original 12 apostles had died. Dallas Theological Seminary even states in their doctrinal statement that these gifts died in the first century.

They state:

We believe that some miraculous manifestations of the Holy Spirit were unique to the apostolic period for the provision of new revelation and the establishment of the authority of the apostles and prophets. Such abilities and confirmatory signs, wonders, and miracles, which centered on individual apostles and prophets, ceased with the passing of these foundational offices and the closing of the era of authoritative New Testament revelation. Even at that time, prophesying and speaking in tongues as signs and sources of revelation were never the common

---

3. Ibid, page780

or necessary mark of the baptism nor of the filling of the Spirit. [4]

So even now, this move of God, restoring the gifts of the Spirit is maligned by former moves of God.

One thing that happened after the Pentecostal movement got well established, was that they began to think that if you didn't have the same gifting and experience as them, then you were second class Christians, if a Christian at all. Many times it was said that God would never save Catholics or mainline denominational churches because they didn't have the experience of the Holy Spirit as they did.

Then in the late 1960's and early 1970's the Holy Spirit began to pour out on Catholics, Lutherans, Episcopalians and other mainline denominations in what became known as the Charismatic movement.

Then the former move, the Pentecostals, began to claim this was not of God because, in their opinion, God wouldn't move in these dry dead churches. But despite their opinion, God did move and didn't ask for their permission.

Priests, Nuns, lay folks all began experiencing various forms of the Holy Spirit's gifts. One good example of this is documented in the book by Episcopal priest Dennis Bennett, *Nine O'clock in the Morn-*

---

4. Board of Incorporate Members' Update on the DTS Doctrinal Statement - Dallas Theological Seminary last accessed November 21, 2024

ing, where a Catholic Priest led him into the Baptism of the Holy Spirit, and this released his Prayer language.[5]

This move of God spread like wildfire around the globe, but persecution, mocking, and even killings chased these groups as they sprung up. But none of this stopped God.

What is of note, is that whenever God brings a new move or truth into the earth, those who embrace it move with what God is currently doing. But those who do not move with God stay stuck in their former move, not moving forward. Thus, there are Holiness churches, such as the Nazarene, Christian Missionary Alliance and others who hang onto the truth they do have but miss out on all they could have. For instance, some of these churches from former moves would now acknowledge that these gifts are real, but do not encourage anyone to seek after them.

5. Bennett, Dennis, *Nine O'Clock in the Morning*, Bridge-Logos, Newberry, Florida 1970, reprint 2017, 2019

Chapter Eight

Women in Ministry

Maria Woodsworth Etter

When we look in the New Testament we see women being used in leadership of the early church. Such examples are Lydia, the business woman, in whose house a church was formed. Priscilla, also taught with her husband and had a church in their house (**1 Corinthians 16:19**). In **Acts 18: 24-26**, *they* took Apollos aside to instruct him more accurately in the way of the Lord. Not just the husband, but both of them.

In **Philippians 4:2-3** we have two women leaders,

I implore **Euodia** and I implore **Syntyche** to be of the same mind in the Lord. [3] And I urge you also, true companion, **help these**

women who labored with me in the gospel, with Clement also, and the rest of my fellow workers, whose names *are* in the Book of Life.

This may not have been true in all of ancient Rome, but in Macedonia women clearly had a leading place in the church.[1]

Yet with the advent of the Dark Ages and the rise of the Roman church from that time period, women were relegated to secondary servant roles. They could be Nuns, but they could not be Priests or consecrate the sacraments.

Yet, God kept moving and restoring what had been lost from His first century church.

Maria Woodworth-Etter, born on a farm, July 22, 1844, in Lisbon Ohio, had a call of God on her life. She heard the call of God on her life to "go into the highways and hedges and gather in the lost sheep". But one thing stopped her. She was a woman, and in the mid nineteenth century, women were not allowed to preach, they were not allowed to vote, so to be a single woman in ministry was out of the question. Nor had Maria ever heard of any woman preaching.[2] She married P.H. Woodworth, a wounded soldier from the Civil War, and they had six children. Her husband had no interest in ministry, and she had six children to raise. Yet this call on her life to preach kept nagging at her. But how could a woman preach? Her husband would never allow it, neither would her children. However, a disease struck 5 of

---

1. Barclay, William, *The Letter to the Philippians, Colossians and Thessalonians*, revised edition, Westminster Press, Philadelphia, 1977, page 73

2. Liardon, Roberts, *God's Generals, Why They Succeeded and Why Some Failed.*, Albury Publishing, Tulsa Oklahoma, 1966, page 47

her children. Leaving her with only one daughter. No sons could now object to their mother preaching. This calamity caused her to seek God even further, and one night, angels came into her room. They showed her a vision of her preaching in the West where multitudes were saved. She humbly answered yes to this call. Her husband did not support this. Maria preached first in her own community. The crowd consisted mostly of her relatives.

God moved and many were reduced to repentant tears. This launched an open door for many churches to call for her to come hold a revival. An unusual sign God performed in her meetings was that people often fell into trances; they would not move, but for a period of time would have visions of the glories of Heaven and of the horrors of Hell and were told to make a decision. One religious man who came to mock and make fun of these signs, fell into a trance himself. Afterwards he declared he had to choose between the two and chose Heaven. He was saved and commented that he was sorry he spent sixty years lost in religion, but never knowing Jesus Christ personally.[3]

Thousands came to Christ in her meetings. She had tents that seated thousands of people, and they would be filled. But as in the past, the former moves of God and even her contemporaries came against what God was doing through His handmaiden. One such contemporary minister was John Alexander Dowie. He publicly blasted her ministry calling it a great delusion, using her as an example of spiritual abuses. [4] Etter simply said wait to see how it all comes out and prophesied that she still will be living when he had died. Dowie died 17 years before Etter.

---

3. Ibid, page 52

4. Ibid, page 59

But otherwise, Maria would not defend herself, just as Jesus kept silent before the Sanhedrin and Pilate at His trial. She let God fight her battles.

As the Lord had led her to the West, she started having meetings in Oakland, California.

But persecution was at every corner. Hoodlums started coming to her meetings to cause chaos and destruction. They hid explosives in the wood stoves, yet miraculously no one was hurt. Some rowdy men were even paid to disrupt her meetings. Yet Maria just trusted God. One man came to her meeting determined to break it up, he stood within ten feet of her platform and cursed a loud string of profanities. Suddenly a power overtook his tongue and he could only say what the Power allowed. Later questioned by two newspaper men, he told them to go up front and find out for themselves.[5]

Additionally, frequently people from insane asylums were brought to her California meetings to disrupt the flow of the Spirit. This happened so many times that it made some people believe, and newspapers report, that her meetings made people insane.[6]

Death threats were weekly events, newspapers and ministers slandered her frequently.

During the Oakland meetings, her husband's infidelity was exposed. After twenty-six difficult years, Maria divorced her husband in January 1891. He quickly remarried and publicly slandered her character and ministry. But the next year, he died of typhoid fever on June 21, 1892.

---

5. Ibid, page 62

6. Ibid, page 58

Despite all these trials, God used her to bring thousands and thousands of souls to Himself. People became healed of impossible things like tuberculosis, and cancers. By the time she reached forty, she was a national phenomenon. [7]

She stirred dead churches, bringing the life of God back into them.

Ten years after her divorce, she met and married a man named Samuel Etter, from Hot Springs Arkansas. Unlike her first husband Mr. Etter fully supported his wife's ministry and was fully engaged in it.

Sept 16, 1924 Mrs. Etter died at 80 years of age. Though women were not allowed to preach, and she was mocked because of it, she obeyed God anyway and left a legacy that followed her into Heaven.

***

Aimee Semple McPherson

After Maria Woodworth-Etter had been a trailblazer for women in ministry, others followed her example. Aimee Semple McPherson was one. She founded and pastored the Angelus Temple in Los Angeles, led thousands of people to the Lord, started LIFE Bible College, and graduated 8,000 ministers from her Bible school.

---

7. Ibid, page 55

Born October 9, 1890, Aimee had her first encounter with the living God when she was 18, in 1908. Women were not allowed to preach, it simply was not done. But God was calling her to win souls for Him. This became a dilemma since women were relegated to secondary positions, like Sunday school teachers. God wouldn't let her off the hook. Large crowds came to hear her because a woman preaching was a novelty, but also because she did not shy away from theatrics which drew in people. She flowed with the Holy Spirit and her ministry grew from tents to coliseums[8]

When she arrived in Los Angeles in 1918, the Azusa Street Mission was now defunct, but the members who had been there quickly flocked to this woman of faith. She knew she had to settle in one location to be the most effective, but until she could afford to build Angelus Temple in Los Angeles, she preached in many other locations. In Baltimore she rented an auditorium which seated 3,000 people, but it was too small for the crowds. So instead, she rented another auditorium that seated sixteen thousand people.

The press had a love/ hate relationship with her and often tried to trip her up. Once she was asked "If silk stockings were a sin". She replied, crossing her legs, that "It depended on how much of them were showing".[9]

---

8. Ibid, page 247

9. Ibid, page 250

Angelus Temple in Los Angeles was completed in 1923; it is considered the first U.S. megachurch. It is still a thriving church, whose attendance is over 8,000 people.[10]

Many Hollywood stars attended the church such as Mary Pickford, Jean Harlow, Charlie Chaplin, and Clara Bow. Anthony Quinn also played in her band.[11]

In 1924 Aimee opened a radio station KFSG with the first FCC license ever issued to a woman and it also was the first Christian radio station in operation.[12]

There is no question that Aimee Semple McPherson's life and ministry was surrounded with controversy, and much could be said about that. However, by the time she passed away on September 27, 1944, at the age of 53, she left behind a remarkable legacy that still lives on.

***

Kathryn Kuhlman

Even though Maria Woodworth-Etter and Aimee Semple McPherson had shown the world what God could do with women in ministry, still great resistance came from Christians. So, next in the way of world-wide, miracle working ministries came Kathryn Kuhlman. She was a strong-willed freckled face girl from Concordia Missouri, born May 9, 1907 and died February 20, 1976 at age 68.

Just after her fourteenth birthday, Kathryn was at a revival held at a local Methodist church. Rev. Hummel, a Baptist evangelist, was preaching there for a two-week meeting.[13] As the minister gave the invitation at the end of Sunday morning's service, Kathryn, though standing with her mother, began to cry. This sobbing became so intense, she began to shake. She dropped her hymnal and ran to the front of the altar, sobbing so loudly she could be heard all over that church. The convicting power of the Holy Spirit had changed her life.[14]

Though her mother went to the local Methodist church, she chose to go to her father's Baptist church. Secondary school in Concordia ended at 10th grade. At sixteen years of age her older sister Myrtle convinced her parents to let Kathryn travel with her and Everett Parrott, her evangelist husband. Reluctantly, her parents consented. Kathryn got on the train with her sister headed for Kansas City, and she knew

---

13. Buckingham, Jamie, *Daughter of Destiny, Kathryn Kuhlman, Her Story*, Bridge Publishing, South , Plainfield, New Jersey, 1976, page 20

14. Ibid, page 22

Concordia would never be her home again. Everett preached under a tent in town after town, wherever he set up meetings.

Everett enjoined another lady, Helen Gulliford, to join his team to sing and play piano. She and Kathryn became fast friends. After travelling with her sister and brother-in-law for several years, a door opened for Kathryn to leave. She and Helen were invited by a local Nazarene pastor in Boise, ID, to help him with a mission church in a run down section of Boise. It had once been a pool hall.[15]

Soon after cutting away from her sister, Kathryn and Helen traveled quite extensively renting locations where they could hold their services. Kathryn had a special gift for recognizing the healing power of the Holy Spirit and called out miracles as they were happening in her services. She would not let them be published as testimonies unless they met the criteria of being instantaneous, not of natural processes, and were documented by a physician. So many people adored her and were thankful for the healing miracles in her services.

But she had critics too. Kathryn had more critics inside the church than outside. People in the world don't care about your denomination or whether you speak in tongues, they care about whether God will touch them. They've tried potions and pills and doctors and demons but only get worse. But if the God of the Universe is in your meetings and touches them where they hurt, they will come. But in the church world, they can go looking for human faults and find reasons to criticize a ministry.[16] Some criticized her because she was a woman, some because she had never been to seminary, some because not everyone who came to her services were healed, though many were.

---

15. Ibid, page 36

16. Ibid, page 42

Some criticized her because she was not perfect, or her theology did not match with that of their understanding.

Thus, Kathryn would always say we have to stay with the Word of God; and not with anything added. [17] She pointed out that she was not perfect, and that she wasn't God. Whom He healed, He healed and as for those not healed, that was up to Him, not her. She said she could not heal a single person. She just preached faith and salvation and let the Holy Spirit do the work He so chose. She never claimed to have great theological training, but said she got her training from the greatest teacher of all, in the school of prayer under the teaching of the Holy Spirit.[18]

In 1933, during the time of the Great Depression, when banks and businesses alike had closed; when people stood in bread lines, Kathryn felt led to go to Denver for miracle services.

She told her assistant, Helen, go up there like we have a million dollars. Rent the biggest building you can, get the finest grand piano to play, rent chairs to fill the hall. Though they had only five dollars, not a million, Kathyrn said if we serve a God who is limited to our finances then we're serving the wrong God. [19]

They got a Montgomery Ward warehouse, filled it with five hundred chairs and a grand piano. They promised to pay these vendors in two weeks after the revival ended. The revival did not end in two weeks, however. It stretched into five years. Many churches reflected the Great Depression, they were lifeless and many even closed.

---

17. Ibid, page 44

18. Ibid, page 48

19. Ibid, page 56

Kathryn instead reflected on the greatness of God. She invited people to come to the banquet hall of God. After five months, Kathryn felt she had been there longer than intended and announced she would leave but the people would not have it. A man jumped up and offered to provide the down payment on the biggest building she could find to establish the Denver Revival Tabernacle. The ministry grew; people were fed, Sunday school for children bussed in children from the area, prison ministry began, ministry to nursing homes began, and many guest preachers came to see what God was doing.

Some of those ministers were even invited to preach, since other than Monday, services were held every single day. But one evangelist invited to speak in 1935, Burroughs A. Waltrip, came and that changed everything, and not for good. This handsome man came from Austin Texas where he had a wife and two little boys. He left that family, began a ministry in Mason City Iowa and presented himself as a single man. He did get a divorce eventually. It was uncontested. But on October 16, 1938 Kathryn announced to her church that she planned to join the ministry with Waltrip in Mason City Iowa. Two days later they were secretly married. It was about sixteen months since Waltrip's divorce.

Helen and another friend went with Kathryn to Mason City to witness the marriage, but both backed out because they kept feeling it was wrong. Kathryn kept saying she couldn't find the will of God on the matter but married him anyway. During the ceremony, Kathryn fainted and Waltrip had to revive her so she could finish her vows.[20]

Instead of going to the hotel with her new husband, she chickened out and went with her friends, Helen and Lottie Anthony. They

20. Liardon, pages 284-285

called Waltrip to say Kuhlman would get an annulment and that the marriage was a mistake.

When they got back to Denver, however, everything exploded. The congregation was furious for her marrying secretly to a divorced man. Another minister bought out Kathryn's part of the building, Helen went to work for a smaller church, and the congregation disintegrated. The congregation's fury drove Kathryn back into Waltrip's arms. She stayed married to this man that she loved until 1944. Kathryn spent the next eight years in oblivion. Six years married to Waltrip and two more years after she left him trying to find her away back to God and His purpose for her. Waltrip finally divorced her in 1947.

Waltrip's ministry also dried up when the congregation discovered he had lied about his first marriage. Once people knew Kathryn was married to a divorced man, meetings were cancelled and no more came forth.

Kathryn once stated that she had to decide between the man she loved and the God she loved. She said while living with Waltrip she also had to live with her conscience.[21]

But if the church world found it hard to accept women in ministry, a divorced woman in ministry was going to be even harder to accept. The former move of God, the church, would no longer accept that God still had plans for her.

- For the gifts and the calling of God *are* irrevocable (**Romans 11:29**. NKJV)

God was not done. Her biggest ministry was yet to begin.

> God was not done. Her biggest ministry was yet to begin.

---

21. Ibid, page 287

As for Waltrip, he met his end in a California prison, convicted of stealing money from a woman.[22] Waltrip passed away in 1949 at the age of 46.

In 1946 Kathyrn was invited to hold a series of meetings in Franklin, Pennsylvania, in the Gospel Tabernacle, a 1500 seat auditorium. The meetings were so anointed it was as if the difficult last eight years never existed. Next, she began a radio program in Oil City, PA that was so well received that she added a station in Pittsburgh, PA.

Though previously Kathryn's focus of ministry was salvation, God began to do miraculous healings as people sat listening to her. So her focus shifted to getting to know the Holy Spirit and His miracles as well as salvation. The healings brought such great responses that she eventually bought a skating rink in Sugar Creek Pennsylvania, near Franklin, and named it Faith Temple. It was twice the size of the building she was renting. It was packed the first night. Over time, God moved on her heart to relocate to Pittsburgh. She was reluctant to leave the Franklin PA area. She said the people of Franklin had been good to her, and for her to move the roof of that skating rink would have to literally fall in. On Thanksgiving, 1950, a huge snow storm caused the collapsed of the roof of that building. Three weeks later, Kathryn moved to the Pittsburgh area.[23]

Kathryn's ministry began expanding. She held regular meetings in Pittsburgh, Pennsylvania, but also Akron Ohio, and Los Angeles California, and wherever other doors would open. Though Kathyrn's ministry began taking her around the nation, and wherever she went

---

22. Ibid, page 288

23. Ibid, page 293

documented healing miracles followed in her meetings, still there were those who insisted on fighting what God was doing. First, because they couldn't believe God would use a woman, and secondly, because they believed God no longer performed miracles. Thy felt God stopped working miracles when the first century apostles died out.

Some of the men who attacked this move of God included John R. Rice and J. Frank Norris of the First Baptist Church of Ft. Worth , Texas.[24] John Rice had written a successful book entitled *Bobbed Hair, Bossy Wives and Women Preachers*.[25] Also ordained from that First Baptist Church of Ft. Worth, Texas, was a preacher named Dallas Billington. In 1925 he moved to Akron Ohio, and in 1934 established the multimillion-dollar Akron Baptist Temple. He ruled over Akron as a spiritual monarch. When a travelling evangelist arrived in Akron with their 15,000 seat tent to hold revivals, Billington went to work to stop it. Rev. Rex Humbard had also invited the faith healer and obvious woman, Kathryn Kulman to join him in the tent revivals. For Billington, this was over the top. He'd have none of that in his city.

On August 10, 1952 Kathryn preached to a crowd of over 15,000 people there in the tent in Akron. On August 15, Billington covered the front page of the Akron Beacon Journal with an offer of $5,000 to anyone who could prove he or she could heal a person through prayer.[26]

Billington declared that:

---

24. Buckingham, page 124

25. Rice, John, *Bobbed Hair, Bossy Wives and Women Preachers, Publisher Sword of the Lord, 2000* (original Jan 1, 1941)

26. Ibid, page 125

"there was no greater racket in America, whether it be horse jockeying, dog races, or the numbers racket, than the so called divine healers of our day. I have a mute class in my congregation. If Kathryn Kuhlman will come to the Temple on Sunday and open their ears and loose their tongues so they can talk, I'll let her hold one service in my Temple each month for twelve months free of charge"[27]

Billington further stated that

"Nowhere was the power of divine healing ever given to be administered by a woman. Women have their rightful places but when you put one in the pulpit it is unscriptural"[28]

Kathyrn responded to the press that she had been in the vicinity for seven years and that her life and ministry speak for themselves.

"I have never at anytime or place made a statement that I have healed anyone. It is the power of God." [29]

The next Sunday when Kathryn came to preach more than 20,000 people lined up to hear her. Billington had inadvertently given Rex Humbard and Kuhlman more free advertising than they could ever have paid for.

Kathryn provided the press with documented healing testimonies of a husband and wife who had been deaf mutes but were now able to hear and speak, though their speech was difficult to understand. Also, another doctor verified the miracle of a woman who was crippled and had been healed in a Kuhlman service. This was also presented to the newspapers.

---

27. Ibid

28. Ibid

29. Ibid, page 126

Subsequently, Rex Humbard stayed in Akron and built a church, The Cathedral of Tomorrow, that became one of the world's largest churches. Kathryn was a frequent guest speaker there.

***

Mildred Wicks

According to Daniel Isgrigg, Ph.D. an Associate Professor and Pentecostal Historian at Oral Roberts University and an Assemblies of God minister for over 20 years, Mildred Wicks was considered one of the most powerful and anointed female ministers in the early Pentecostal Healing movement. [30] Mildred Wicks was born in New Mexico on May 3, 1913, but her family moved to Oklahoma where she was raised. At age eighteen she was filled with the Holy Spirit at an Assemblies of God camp meeting on August 9, 1931. Then a few months later, Wicks preached her first revival in which nearly 200 people came to Christ. She was licensed under the Pentecostal Holiness Church as a pastor and evangelist and over the next decade she pastored churches across Oklahoma, including Woodville, Cromwell, Kiowa, and Westville.

In 1938, Mildred Wicks was chosen as pastor of the Pentecostal Holi-

---

30. https://danieldisgrigg.com/2022/05/08/mildred-wicks/
    Last accessed August 24, 2024.

ness Church in Westville, a small town on the Eastern border of Oklahoma on the route from Siloam Springs to Muskogee. Oral Roberts' father, Ellis Roberts, pastored the church for a year before Wicks came to be the pastor.

As one of her biggest fans, Oral Roberts commented,

> "I have never heard any better or more inspired preaching than was delivered by Sister Wicks. Her deeply spiritual ministry, her intensely prayerful life, her queenly walk and anointed sermons served to break down prejudice, indifference, lukewarmness and persecution and led the way for a soul ingathering revival."[31]

In 1947, Roberts and Wicks teamed up since they were invited to hold healing crusades in Newnan, Georgia, at a church they both had pastored. The pastor called it "the greatest revival in the history of the Newnan church." Together, they ministered to the crowd of over 700 people nightly, laying hands on the sick in a healing line that stretched around the building for hours. This service demonstrated that both would to be leaders in the healing ministry. [32]

By 1953, Wicks joined Gordon Lindsey's Voice of Healing collective of Healing Revivalists as one of two women actively promoted in the *Voice of Healing* magazine. She was also touted as one of the

---

30. https://danieldisgrigg.com/2022/05/08/mildred-wicks/
Last accessed August 24, 2024.

31. Ibid

32. Ibid

"greatest women evangelists" by Jack Coe and the only female preacher he promoted.[33]

So, Mildred Wicks was a part of two moves of God: The Pentecostal Holiness movement and the Move of God among Women in ministry.

She died in 1998 but in her later years she visited and preached at the LGBT (+) affirming **Advance Christian Conference.** (See *The Holy Spirit and the Gay Community*.)[34]

***

Rev. Doris Swartz (Dayton, Ohio)

Despite the powerful pastoral ministries woman have had with signs, wonders and miracles accompanying their services, still segments of the Church find themselves fighting God on this.

God ordained the women mentioned earlier, yet even with all the documentation and proof that the Holy Spirit has been at work, others from previous moves of God refuse to accept this as a sovereign work.

The Southern Baptist convention has adamantly insisted women cannot pastor a church. Certainly not as a senior pastor because, they say, this role can *only* be occupied by men.

---

33. Ibid

34. Kader, Samuel, The Holy Spirit and the Gay Community, the Early Years, SK Ministry, 2014

NBC news reported on June 14, 2023 that the Southern Baptist Convention overwhelmingly voted to oust churches who allowed women to be pastors.

NBC news noted:

Spurred on by arch-conservatives in the SBC, the 12,000 or so "messengers" who had gathered at their annual meeting in New Orleans voted by a 9-to-1 ratio to seal the exit of California's Saddleback Church and a smaller congregation in Kentucky.

The vote... set the stage for another vote ...to amend the SBC's constitution to specify that Southern Baptist churches must "affirm, appoint or employ only men as any kind of pastor or elder as qualified by Scripture."

That, too, passed with a two-thirds majority.

Sarah Clatworthy, a member of Lifepoint Baptist Church in San Angelo, Texas, who has called on the SBC "to shut the door to feminism and liberalism," said she supported the ban on female pastors.

"We should leave no room for our daughters and granddaughters in the generations ahead to have confusion on where the SBC stands,". "Let them know Scripture is our authority and not the culture."

Earlier, SBC President Bart Barber defended the vote to expel the churches and noted that the Roman Catholic Church also does not allow women to serve as pastors or priests.

"We believe that every believer is a priest," Barber said. "We have women who served as messengers. It's just the Scriptures say the office of pastor is limited to men."

Saddleback Church, a megachurch based in Southern California with a flock of around 23,000, was founded by Rick Warren, the author of the bestselling phenomenon "*The Purpose Driven Life.*"

The church drew the ire of the Southern Baptist Convention when it accepted women as pastors in 2021.

But the vote to declare Saddleback "not to be in friendly cooperation" with the denomination was due to "the church continuing to have a female teaching pastor functioning in the office of a pastor," the SBC said in a statement."[35]

Also noted for pastoring **United Christian Center**, a Pentecostal church in Dayton Ohio, **Rev. Doris Swartz** led a thriving congregation. She also was the president of a network of international Pentecostal churches called the International Ministers Forum. They held annual conventions hosted in Dayton at her church.

Pastor Doris was effective and beloved as a pastor, and opened the door for many thriving ministries around the world. She and her church often made trips to Honduras to establish and support ministries, churches, schools and clinics that could only be reached by bus on rugged dirt roads and then by canoe. She had purchased a historic large Methodist inner-city church in Dayton as her base, but prior to purchasing the building, her church rented it from the Methodists. One day, while walking through the large social hall, there was a group of male Methodist ministers having a meeting. As she walked through the room, the men asked her what she thought about

---

35. NBC news: _Southern Baptists vote to expel two churches led by female pastors_

June 14, 2023, 12:35 PM EDT / Updated June 14, 2023, 4:43 PM EDT By Corky Siemaszko

last accessed 1/5/2025

women in ministry. Pastor Doris replied, "I'm sorry , but I don't deal in elementary education."

> **Pastor Doris replied, "I'm sorry but I don't deal in elementary education."**

Still, the Southern Baptist Convention, the largest Christian denomination in America, will not accept or recognize these powerfully anointed women as pastors of churches. Fortunately for these anointed women of God, they did not need the blessing from the SBC to flow in what God called them to do[36] . Still, the former move of God (SBC flows with the Anabaptist theology) fights what God is doing.

In Acts chapter ten, the Apostle Peter sees a vision of a sheet being lowered. On it are all the animals that are not kosher and are forbidden by Jewish law to be eaten. Then in this vision God tells him to eat these. But it was God who put the rules in place through Moses. Then gentiles come to call for Peter to go with them to the house of a Roman centurion. This is a non Jew. It is illegal to go to his house per kosher laws. He is a Roman soldier, part of the occupying force; he is the enemy of Israel. Yet God tells Peter to go with them to the house of Cornelius. When Peter arrives at the house of this Roman centurion, this uncircumcised gentile, as God had instructed, as he tells them about Jesus and the Cross, the Holy Spirit falls upon these Romans and baptizes them in the Spirit. It is then that Peter realizes that the rules have changed. God is doing a new thing.

In the New Testament Paul tells women to be silent in the church, and to submit to their husbands. People say they want to return to Biblical sexual ethics. But really, that condones polygamy, (Solomon

---

36. Galatians 3: 28

had 700 wives and 300 concubines[37]). But by the same token he tells slaves to submit to their masters. There are 326 verses that relate to slaves and slavery.[38] Those passages were used to perpetuate the slave trade in America.[39] It took 1700 years for Christians to change their thinking about slavery. The rules changed. Wilberforce, Wesley and many others began to get a revelation that there was a broader application of Scripture: that people were created equal.

As far as the Scriptural references to women in the Bible, do those passages represent God's plan for woman for all of time or are they culturally conditioned based on the times in which the churches were being instructed? Well, it was also Paul who said that in Christ there is neither male nor female in Christ Jesus.[40] In the last few centuries God has raised many anointed women as preachers, evangelists, and senior pastors of churches. The rules have changed. But as in other new things God is doing, the former move fights the current move of God. In these cases, the Church finds itself on the wrong side of history, despite how many political strings they can pull or how loudly they can shout. It was the religious right of Jesus day, the Moses followers, who shouted the loudest: "Crucify Him, Crucify Him!" and though they got their way, they were fighting God and lost.

---

37. 1 Kings 11:3

38. Hamilton, Adam, "*When Christians Get it Wrong, Politics, Judgment, Salvation, Sexuality, Tragedy,* Science"; Abingdon Press, Nashville, 2013, page 84

39. ibid

40. Galatians 3:28

Despite the objections some mainline Christian groups have against women as pastors and in ministry, God keeps moving forward with His daughters, without asking for permission. Even within the Catholic church, a group has arisen; Roman Catholic Women Priests[41] . Their web page identifies them as " A New Model of Ordained Ministry in a Renewed Roman Catholic Church". Nonetheless, the pope has declared this as heresy. Despite his consternation, these women do hold mass, consecrate communion, and pastor churches. Two such women were a regular part of our local church at one time, Rev. Ronnie Dubignon, and Rev. Eleonora Marinaro, and their ordination was accepted and celebrated within our Charismatic Affirming church; New Life Community Gospel Church in New Port Richey, Florida.

Chapter Nine

The Move of the Holy Spirit among the Hippies.

U p until the late 1960's, Pentecostal churches were the only known Holy Spirit filled churches where the gifts of the Spirit were manifested, particularly speaking in tongues and prophecy. As a result, some Pentecostal churches began to be puffed up with pride. They would frequently declare that the denominational liturgical churches were dead dry bones and had no life. They often would even declare that these cold stone-dead churches would not make it to Heaven, because they did not have the Holy Spirit manifested as they did. In particular they were certain God would never save Catholics,

Lutherans, Presbyterians, or Episcopalians. In their mindset these folks were beyond God's redemption.

Then God stepped in.

Reverend Dennis Bennett was praying and asking God for a deeper walk with Him. A Catholic priest who was listening to the leading of the Holy Spirit dropped in on Rev. Bennett and led him into the baptism of the Holy Spirit, evidenced by releasing his prayer language, speaking in tongues. After this event, Rev. Bennett who was the rector of St. Mark's Episcopal Church in Van Nuys, California, told his congregation about his Pentecostal experience. They did not approve of this announcement and he was forced to resign. This event, however, attributed to April 3, 1960 is generally considered to have been the beginning of the Charismatic movement. Rev. Dennis J. Bennett wrote of this experience in his now famous book *"Nine O'clock in the Morning"* [1]

By 1962 Lutherans and Presbyterians were experiencing this move of the Holy Spirit, and the Catholic Church began seeing this outpouring beginning in 1967 at Duquesne University in Pittsburgh, Pennsylvania as well as at Notre Dame University in South Bend, Indiana. Methodists also joined the Charismatic revival in the 1970's. Unlike the Pentecostals, whose emphasis was on speaking in tongues as the proof one had been filled with the Holy Spirit, the Charismatic renewal embraced many of the gifts of the Spirit listed in 1 Corinthians 12, and especially healing.

Because Pentecostals would not believe God would move through and fill these historic denominations, they initially rejected the

---

1. Bennett, Dennis, *"Nine O'clock in the Morning"*, Bridge-Logos, Inc. (June 20, 2011)

Charismatic revival within these churches. I personally heard many Pentecostal preachers condemn the Charismatic movement as not from God. Here again we had the former move of God fighting the new move of God. It upset their religious ideology. Then there were other Christian groups, such as the Southern Baptist Convention whose theology would not accommodate any such display of the Holy Spirit. And just as they rejected the Pentecostal movement, so they rejected the Charismatic movement. Thus, many former Baptists who received the infilling of the Holy Spirit had to leave the Baptist church and begin their own congregations. These became the Charismatic churches that exist today. Yet God did not quit or reject His Baptist children. He still filled many of them with the Holy Spirit and with gifts such as tongues. But if they wanted to remain in the Southern Baptist church they had to stay in the closet about this relationship they now had with God's Holy Spirit. Many students in the 1970's who attended Dallas Theological Seminary and spoke in tongues were subsequently expelled. This may still be the case.

***

Lonnie Frisbee

Born June 6, 1949, Lonnie Frisbee was a young hippie living in the Haight-Asbury area of San Francisco in the late 1960's. Yet, God used this young man to revolutionize the young people of his day, becoming a major catalyst for the Jesus movement of the 1970's. Yet no one would probably identify Lonnie with this movement until film maker, David Di Sabatino released the DVD "*Frisbee: the Life and Death of a Hippie Preacher*."

At seventeen years of age, Frisbee went to a lone wilderness canyon in California and cried out to God: "If You're really real, reveal Yourself to me!" He said the atmosphere began to change and he had a vision of thousands of young people being baptized in the ocean. When he returned to the Haight Asbury that day in 1967, he was changed. A mission in the area had a drop in center for the homeless hippies living on the street and became a mentoring place for young Frisbee. By eighteen Lonnie was a powerful street evangelist in the Haight-Asbury area, leading other young people to Christ.

Lonnie made a few journeys to southern California where he connected with a small storefront ministry called Teen Challenge that ministered to drug addicts and homeless people. [2] The leader's name was Bob, and he took Lonnie to Fullerton Foursquare Church, (of the denomination founded by Aimee Semple McPherson) where he could receive the Baptism of the Holy Spirit and have his private prayer language (tongues) released. Frisbee would go to the beaches of Southern California at Newport Pier and just begin to preach. A crowd would soon draw near him. It was easy for Lonnie to then baptize them in the Pacific Ocean.

Back in the Haight-Asbury, a Mission drop-in center had also created a commune, the Novato ranch called the House of Acts. Five

---

2. Howard, Lee Allen "*Lonnie Frisbee Catalyst for Revival, the New Move of the Holy Spirit, from Hippies to Homosexuals*", Acceptable Books, Jamestown NY, 2016. Page 23

families lived together there for two years[3]. Of those invited to live at the commune was a troubled girl named Connie Bremer. Lonnie had led her to the Lord when she was on an acid trip in a Canyon. They married in April 1968. Many more details are contained in Howard's book[4] as well as the three volume books Lonnie Frisbee himself wrote with Roger Sachs.

Nevertheless, Lonnie would still travel from San Francisco to Southern California, hitchhiking along the way. He found this to be an effective way to evangelize people who gave him a ride. He had a soft, easy manner. He was not a loud preacher, but serious and conversational. He also loved to start conversations with hippies about Jesus in the Haight. He sympathized with those who had a hard life because his early years were also fraught with abuse. He could relate, and his heart went out to them.

Those who lived at the commune noticed that Lonnie was not particularly affectionate with his wife, Connie, though affection was exactly what she needed. She married him when he proposed because he was the first person to ask. She thought of him as a clown, at first, but soon she saw that this "ungroovy clown did strange and powerful things in the Name of Jesus Christ."[5] Lonnie's long brown hair and equally long beard, along with his flowing long robes made him appear as a modern day Jesus. It drew the hippies of his generation to him,

---

3. Frisbee, Lonnie, with Sachs, Roger; "*The Jesus Revolution, Part One, Not by Might, Nor by Power*", Freedom Publications, Santa Maria, CA, second edition 2017, page 65

4. Ibid

5. Howard, page 25

if not out of curiosity. But people got healed, they got saved and baptized, people got filled with the Holy Spirit, and their lives were forever changed by the anointing that God had on this young hippie preacher.

In Lonnie's own testimony, he stated:

> " I would hitchhike down to Southern California, to witness to my family, to people I went to school with, and to anyone. ...I'd go to the Orange County Fair, get out in the middle of an open area and yell, 'HEY!' I'd jump and down and look like a freak. I could draw hundreds of people like that and always felt the anointing of God fall on me when I stepped out in boldness like that. I'd preach and give an altar call before the police got there! Sometimes I'd go to the Newport Pier dressed like a hippie and again yell, 'HEY!' I'd jump up and down with my hair flying in the wind. People would gather around the crazy man. Then I'd preach the gospel, God would put something on it, I'd give an altar call, and fifty people in bathing suits and bikinis would accept the Lord. It was really wonderful!"[6]

***

6. Frisbee, Lonnie, *The Jesus Revolution, part one*, page 66

Chuck Smith of Calvary Chapel

One day Lonnie Frisbee was again hitchhiking to Southern California, when he was picked up by a clean cut, short haired young man. The driver began to share Christ with Lonnie, assuming that a long haired, bearded man was not yet saved. Lonnie interrupted him asking, "Are you trying to get me saved? When the driver said yes, Lonnie said that this was what he did, hitchhiking and sharing the gospel. Lonnie had to do some strong convincing to get the driver to believe he too was a Christian. Lonnie pulled out his bible and the two of them shared Scriptures. Eventually, the driver, John Nicholson, asked Lonnie if it would be OK if he took him to meet someone. Lonnie agreed.

They went to the middle-class Orange County home of Pastor Chuck Smith. John Nicholson was dating Pastor Chuck's daughter. Chuck Smith had a small church of 25 people or so and had a burden to reach out to the thousands of Hippies in Southern California. After a long discussion, Pastor Smith was convinced that Lonnie would be an answer to a prayer. Pastor Chuck proposed that Lonnie and John could team up with Pastor Chuck, and share Christ with the hippies on the beach. Especially since Lonnie spoke their language and understood them. Lonnie liked the idea, but said he lived in San Francisco and was married. Chuck told him to bring his wife and they could stay in their home to begin with.

Eventually Chuck Smith's church, Calvary Chapel, provided a place for Lonnie and Connie to live, which also became another commune for some of the people who got saved on the beach. It was named the House of Miracles. But Connie was not willing to leave the House of Acts commune in Novato. A big fight ensued, but Lonnie was certain of this call, especially once they got a call from Chuck Smith offering to put Lonnie on staff at Calvary Chapel. Connie threatened that if he made her move, she would make him sorry for the rest of his life. According to Lonnie, that's what happened, too.[7]

Once in Southern California, young people began to fill Calvary Chapel. They came as they were, barefooted, and just sat on the floor, rather than in the pews. Some of the elders in the church had a problem with this and complained to pastor Chuck that their bare feet would soil the carpet. Thus Smith had the carpet removed. He wasn't going to let complaints like that put a clamp on the move of God.

Lonnie and his team would preach and pray with people on the beach, and many were brought home with them to the two-bedroom House of Miracles. People slept on the couch, in the hallway, in the garage, and camped in the backyard. Bible studies were held in the home, and these new babes in Christ would be transported to church on Sundays. Then they took the new believers back to the beaches so they, too could give witness to a loving God who rescued them.[8] Several other homes were opened for these new believers, as well as a converted motel.

The church was growing so fast as hundreds and hundreds of young people were getting healed, getting off drugs, and delivered from many other things. As a result of the obvious change in their children, parents also started coming to church. It wasn't long before the church now had a regular attendance of a thousand people. At the beaches, people were getting saved, then getting baptized in the ocean. As their friends came to see them get baptized, they too would get

---

7. Frisbee, *"The Jesus Revolution, Part One"*, page 68

8. Ibid page 69

saved then baptized minutes later. Sunday services moved to two times on Sunday, then three, then they outgrew the building altogether.

Music and musicians began to spring up in this new move of God as well, such as: Children of the Day, Barry McGuire, Andre Crouch, Keith Green, 2nd Chapter of Acts and many others. Yet, even still around America, this new move of God was rejected by older line denominations. I would see billboards that said, "Clean up America – get a haircut!" Churches who rejected these long haired youth became dry and stagnant. Those who embraced them became a part of this Jesus Movement. Thousands of young people were swept into God's kingdom in city after city.

Being part of the staff, as the youth pastor of Calvary Chapel, opened so many more doors for ministry than hitchhiking had ever done. Kay Smith, Chuck Smith's wife prophesied that Lonnie and Connie would have a world wide impact in their ministry.[9] This proved to be true, as time moved forward. They were invited and held meetings in many places in Europe, South Africa, and other parts of the world. One of the people who heard Lonnie preach on his Harbor High School campus was Greg Laurie. He believed the Word Lonnie preached, that Jesus is real, and you can get to know Him now. He said that with Jesus you are either for Him or against Him. There is no middle ground. Laurie came forward and got saved and filled with the Holy Spirit. He followed Lonnie around from meeting after meeting after that. Eventually Greg Laurie would become a pastor himself,

---

9. Howard, *"Catalyst for Revival"*, page 39

and he founded the 15,000 member Harvest Christian Fellowship in Riverside California.[10]

But the local church kept exploding. Kathy Baldock reports that "between 1968 and 1971 Frisbee brought several thousand converts to Calvary Chapel."[11]

Smith had Lonnie minister on Wednesday nights, while Smith took charge of the Sunday services. Lonnie wrote that every seat was filled, the aisles and the front were filled with young people sitting on the floor and the the outside was full of people listening on speakers and looking in the windows. [12] At one of those Wednesday night meetings, unbeknownst to Lonnie, his mother showed up. At first though she was hesitant to go forward for the altar call, but she suddenly saw her son lit up in light with three rainbows emanating from him. She received Christ on the spot.[13]

***

---

10. 14, 560 members and four campuses in different cities. (As of 2022) per Harvest Christian Fellowship numbers reported in Wikipedia. Harvest Christian Fellowship remains a part of the Calvary Chapel network of churches.

11. Baldock, Kathy, *Walking the Bridgeless Canyon, Repairing the Breach Between the Church and the LGBTQ Community*, Canyon Walker Press, Reno, NV. page 352

12. Howard, page 53

13. Ibid, page 55

The Breakup Between Calvary Chapel and Lonnie Frisbee

Chuck Smith was uncomfortable with the physical manifestations that came along with the outpouring of the Holy Spirit during the Jesus movement. He told Lonnie, whose anointing ushered in the presence of the Holy Spirit, that tongues and prophecy were not allowed in the main Sunday service. He further told Lonnie, if you pray for people and they fall down, you're going to lose your job.[14] Additionally, according to Lonnie, he was paid only $25/ week, which for a married couple made them eligible for food stamps. This disparity and the theological disagreements led Lonnie and Connie Frisbee to leave Calvary Chapel in 1971. Soon after the Frisbees moved to Florida to join a ministry to help them work on their fractured marriage. After that year, they moved back to Southern California, about which Connie stated that Kay Smith and Connie Frisbee shopped at the same grocery store, except that Kay went through the front door, and Connie went around back to see what was in the dumpster.[15]

Despite all their efforts, the Frisbees ended their marriage in divorce in 1973. Partly because the ministry took up so much of Lonnie's time that Connie felt neglected and unloved, and partly because she ended up having open adulterous affairs, and partly because Lonnie sometimes spent late nights at gay bars. After three years went by, they ran into each other again and remained friends.

---

14. Ibid pages 61-62

15. Ibid, page 63, 73

Five years after leaving Calvary Chapel, Lonnie decided to go back and make amends with Pastor Chuck Smith. In those prevailing years, Calvary Chapel had transformed into a movement; they had thousands of members, a new building and hundreds of satellite churches being opened or coming under their umbrella. Smith brought Lonnie back on staff as an associate pastor, to run the tape ministry, but warned him that the latitude he once had in the realm of the Spirit would no longer be tolerated.[16] Frisbee was now wearing a three piece suit and had a haircut; but his homosexuality did not go away. Once Smith discovered that Frisbee was still gay, the relationship was irreparably severed.

***

John Wimber, The Vineyard Churches

John Wimber was also a Calvary Chapel minister pastoring one of the satellite churches. But Wimber and Smith
had a major disagreement on the place and ministry of
the Holy Spirit. Smith wanted everything under control
and respectable. Wimber on the other hand, in reading
the book of Acts, wanted to know as a Christian, when
we get to "see the stuff", meaning he had a burning
desire to see the Holy Spirit work in his church. Wimber
helped another pastor, Kenn Gulliksen establish Vineyard Christian Fellowship. [17] They wanted to see the
Holy Spirit be free and active in their group.

On Mother's Day, 1980, John Wimber invited Lonnie Frisbee
to preach in his church. As Lonnie preached, an explosion of the
presence of the Holy Spirit catapulted that Vineyard church into a

---

17. Baldock, page 355

full-blown revival. Lonnie asked all the young people to come forward, and when they did they fell under the power and presence of God. Some older elders of the church walked out in disgust, and the next day Wimber was called into a meeting to explain himself. But during the meeting, Lonnie Frisbee bolted in and pointed at one of the objecting elders. He declared "You need to have the experience with God!"[18] The elder shook uncontrollably and fell to the floor under the power of the Holy Spirit.[19]

The newly saved young people now began to preach to their friends in High School and Junior High, and baptize them in pools and hot tubs. Within six months, with Lonnie preaching and teaching in Wimber's church, the congregation grew from 500 to 2500.[20] This was the beginning of the Vineyard church movement.

***

It All Unravels

One day, Chuck Smith Jr. was having lunch with John Wimber. He asked Wimber how he was able to reconcile Lonnie's homosexuality

---

18. Baldock, page 355

19. Ibid

20. Ibid

with the ministry. Apparently, Smith Jr. in a conversation with a pastor friend told Smith that a young man in his church confessed to a six-month homosexual affair with Frisbee. Wimber had no idea about this and immediately fired Lonnie Frisbee.

The Calvary Chapel movement and the Vineyard movement each soon had about one thousand churches. The catalyst and common denominator was Lonnie Frisbee, the Hippie Preacher. But when Calvary Chapel's history was written, Lonnie was not even mentioned. The Vineyard churches did the same thing. Had it not been for the documentary of filmmaker David Di Sabatino[21] Frisbee would be lost to history. Yet some years later, Frisbee was invited to preach in Sweden, Denmark, and South Africa. Revival still followed him wherever he went. The anointing that God gave Lonnie was active and alive. Did God not know Frisbee was gay when He called him?

> Did God not know Frisbee was gay when He called him?

Of course He did.

Lonnie could have done much more for the Kingdom of God as well, had the church not fought God. But instead Lonnie died of AIDS complications in 1993. Frisbee was interred in the Crystal Cathedral Memorial Gardens, in Southern California. I believe this was another instance of when the church fought God, even when He was moving so powerfully through His child.

---

21. Di Sabatino, David, _The Life and Death of a Hippie Preacher_ (2006)

Chapter Ten

The Current Move of God – the Eunuchs

I n the gospel of John, chapter ten Jesus tells his disciples that He has other sheep that He must bring in.[1] He doesn't tell who these other sheep might be, He doesn't say anything else about them, except that they also are His, and that He must bring them in. Likewise, He tells them that just as they know His voice, so will these others know His voice. Additionally, as He brings these others into His fold, there will be one fold with one Shepherd. As millions of Hippies became Christians and joined churches, or founded new Charismatic churches, eventually the Jesus movement was accepted as a bona fide

---

1. John 10: 14-16

move of God. But Jesus still has others that He wants to bring in. He did not explain who they might be.

THE WEDDING FEAST

Matthew 22:2-10

2 "The kingdom of heaven is like a certain king who arranged a marriage for his son, 3 and sent out his servants to call those who were invited to the wedding; and they were not willing to come. 4 Again, he sent out other servants, saying, 'Tell those who are invited, "See, I have prepared my dinner; my oxen and fatted cattle *are* killed, and all things *are* ready. Come to the wedding." ' 5 But they made light of it and went their ways, one to his own farm, another to his business. 6 And the rest seized his servants, treated *them* spitefully, and killed *them*. 7 But when the king heard *about it,* he was furious. And he sent out his armies, destroyed those murderers, and burned up their city. 8 Then he said to his servants, 'The wedding is ready, but those who were invited were not worthy. 9 Therefore go into the highways, and as many as you find, invite to the wedding.' 10 So those servants went and gathered together all whom they found, both bad and good. And the wedding *hall* was filled

Matthew 22:8-9

8 Then he said to his servants, 'The wedding is ready, but those who were invited were not worthy. 9 Therefore **go into the highways**, and as many as you find, **invite to the wedding**.

God wants His Kingdom filled. He continually invites people to come. Some choose not to because God doesn't fit into their plans. So, He keeps reaching out to those *others* that Jesus talked about. Those who were a part of a former move of God aren't always happy that God is doing a new thing. But it must be done nonetheless. A new thing, new wine, requires a new vessel, a new wine skin, because the old wine skin can't contain this fresh wine. Otherwise, both will burst. Those in the former move don't want to embrace this new change. They say, the old is good enough.

And with every new move of God a point person has to be anointed to lead this wave of revival. Moses was that anointed point person. Luther was that point person. Maria Woodworth-Etter was that point person. Yet in their generation, they were all rejected by the former move of God.

***

Eunuchs are Us

October 1968 – Now enters Rev. Troy D. Perry – God always uses a point person in a specific moment in time. This was it.

Starting in 1968 the Holy Spirit began hovering over the deep darkness of the gay community. Though there had been sparks here and there prior to that time, but October 1968 is easily identified as the time the fire burst into a blaze that is still encompassing the world. No one can tell the story of the gay Christian movement without telling the story of the father and founder of the movement. **Rev. Troy D. Perry** is the catalyst and point person God used to open this closed harvest field. In God's timing this move was working simultaneously with the Charismatic Movement. Rev. Perry was a Pentecostal minister with a wife and family. But he could not hide the nagging truth that he was in fact gay. Once that truth came out, he lost his church, he lost his family as they moved out, and for a time he did not know what to do or where to go. His mother lived in Huntington Park, California, so until he could get on his feet, he lived with her. Perry had a boyfriend for a time, once he was on his own, and when that relationship broke up, he felt he couldn't go on. He attempted suicide by cutting his wrists in his bathtub. [2] Before it was too late, his neighbors rescued him and got him to a hospital. While there an unknown black woman slapped a magazine into his hands and said, "Some of us care!" This jolted him back to reality and from feeling sorry for himself. As he recovered and went back to work, he ran into a stranger who just prophesied over him that he was a minister and that he'd soon be ministering again[3]. Perry didn't see how that was possible. But as God kept stirring the possibility in his soul, Perry knew he'd have to start a church that was welcoming and affirming for the LGBTQ (+) community. It would have to be for them and by them. Once he convinced his roommate, that this was an undeniable calling on his life, they agreed to start having church services in their home. Thus, in October 1968, the first Metropolitan Community Church was birthed in Los Angeles. Although the Metropolitan Community Churches were the first gay friendly churches on the scene, it wasn't long before many other independent churches within the gay community arose as well. These church homes were needed if gay people and their supporters would ever be welcome into the family of God. Jesus was wooing His *others*. Almost overnight, after that first service with 12 people in

---

2. Perry, Rev. Troy, *The Lord is My Shepherd and He Knows I'm Gay*, Bantam Books, NY, NY 1973 page 97

3. ibid, page 103

Perry's living room, more Metropolitan Community Churches were birthed around the nation.

According to Rev. Troy Perry's web site, the denomination that Perry founded became the largest Affirming organization in the word. It reports:

"Rev. Troy Perry's visionary step in the creation of the first Metropolitan Community Church in 1968 would be historic: the first church to recognize the need to minister to the needs of gays, lesbians, bisexuals and transgender people. Despite fire bombings of its sanctuaries and murders of its clergy, Rev. Troy Perry has led this movement and the expansion of the denomination to become one of the world's largest LGBT organizations with hundreds of churches in countries around the world."[4]

But since gay folks with any Christian religious background whatsoever were coming to these churches, they took on a more ecumenical Christian flavor.

God began moving by His Holy Spirit in the midst of the gay community about the same time as He began moving among the youth counter culture of the 1960's. Hippies began experiencing God in a whole new way, as the Jesus movement sprung up in the late 1960's. At that time many church goers thought Hippies were too far gone for God to reach. Without Church help or approval, God brought them into His Kingdom anyway. Even so, many found they were not welcome in the staid and proper churches of the 1960's. As a result all new churches sprung up on the horizon, and thus many of the independent charismatic churches were birthed.

---

4. https://revtroyperry.com/ last accessed 3/6/2025

At the same time, another group found themselves being wooed by Almighty God. Gays also discovered that they were not welcome in the anti-gay conservative churches they had been raised in. So again, all new churches were birthed beginning in the late 1960's where gay people and their supporters could freely worship God without fear. Jesus said

"And other sheep I have which are not of this fold; them also I must bring, and they will hear My voice; and there will be one flock and one shepherd." John 10:16 (New King James)

This is further stated in the New Testament in **Ephesians 2:13-22**

13. But now in Christ Jesus you who once were far off have been made near by the blood of Christ. 14. For He Himself is our peace, who has made both one, and has broken down the middle wall of division between us, 15. having abolished in His flesh the enmity, that is, the law of commandments contained in ordinances, so as to create in Himself one new man from the two, thus making peace, 16. and that He might reconcile them both to God in one body through the cross, thereby putting to death the enmity. 17. And He came and preached peace to you who were afar off and to those who were near. 18. For through Him we both have access by one Spirit to the Father. 19. Now, therefore, you are no longer strangers and foreigners, but fellow citizens with the saints and members of the household of God, 20. having been built on the foundation of the apostles and prophets, Jesus Christ Himself being the chief cornerstone, 21. in whom the whole building, being joined together, grows into a holy temple in the Lord, 22. in whom you also are being built together for a habitation of God in the Spirit.

Now the immediate problem was that for centuries Christians had taken six Biblical passages to say that God hates LGBT(+) people. What do those passages mean, since the church world was convinced that God hated gays on the one hand, and on the other, here He was saving them, baptizing them, filling them with the gifts and fruit of the Holy Spirit. There was a disconnect. But just like Martin Luther, who suddenly saw a Scripture that revealed what was really on God's heart – "the just shall live by faith", so it was that God began to open the scriptures up to reveal how He loves and not hates His LGBT(+) children. So many books are now available to show this, including my own: *Openly Gay, Openly Christian, How the Bible Really is Gay Friendly.* [5]

Gaychurch.org lists the thousands of affirming churches that now encircle the globe, and is where a local church can be discovered online [6]

So, though the Metropolitan Community Churches were the first on the scene as affirming Christian churches, there are many other affirming denominations and fellowship groups. One powerful example is **the Covenant Network**[7] , a largest network of Spirit filled Christian believers, which is headquartered in Atlanta, Georgia, and

---

5. Kader, Rev. Samuel, *Openly Gay, Openly Christian, How the Bible Really is Gay Friendly,* SK Ministry Inc, 2014

6. https://www.gaychurch.org/
   lists LGBTQ(+) affirming churches that have been verified as being open and affirming. They are listed by nation, then region (ie. States, Province, etc.) and locality.

7. https://www.thecovenantnetwork.com/

which hosts an annual conference called **Immersed** [8] Bishop Randy Morgan is the overseer of that organization. He also pastors a Spirit filled LGBTQ (+) affirming church in Atlanta called New Covenant Church of Atlanta. He is the founder and Bishop of that church since 2000 A.D. Other organizations and fellowship groups have been around for decades as well. Including **Reconciling Pentecostals**,[9] whose Chief Presiding Presbyter is Rev. Daniel Parnell of Indianapolis Indiana; **The Affirming Christian Fellowship** Conference [10] (formerly called TEN-the Evangelical Network); the **All Nations Gathering** hosted in Bellflower California by The Glory Center where Rev. Sandra Turnbull is the Pastor. All these have been bringing life and hope to those hurt and downtrodden by the former moves of God. They continue to bring fresh anointing to a downtrodden and forgotten people who Jesus desires to have within His Kingdom.

As God revealed His love for His LGBTQ(+) children, a Scripture to describe this move of God surfaced; It was John 3:16;

John 3:16

16 For God so loved the world that He gave His only begotten Son, that **WHOEVER** believes in Him should not perish but have everlasting life.

---

8. https://www.theimmersedconference.com/ the Immersed Conference is an annual conference held in Atlanta Georgia where Christian Spirit Filled LGBT (+) allies gather for worship and fellowship.

9. https://rpifellowship.com/

10. https://www.facebook.com/AffirmingChristianFellowship

WHOEVER means whoever. Whoever believes. That's it. Additionally, God showed those within this move of God the term He used in Scripture to identify His sexual minority folks. It was the term **Eunuch**. Look at the following Scripture:

Matthew 19:3-12

³ The Pharisees also came to Him, testing Him, and saying to Him, "Is it lawful for a man to divorce his wife for *just* any reason?"

⁴ And He answered and said to them, "Have you not read that He who made *them* at the beginning 'made them male and female,' ⁵ and said, 'For this reason a man shall leave his father and mother and be joined to his wife, and the two shall become one flesh'? ⁶ So then, they are no longer two but one flesh. Therefore what God has joined together, let not man separate."

⁷ They said to Him, "**Why then did Moses command to give a certificate of divorce, and to put her away?**"

⁸ He said to them, "Moses, because of the hardness of your hearts, permitted you to divorce your wives, but from the beginning it was not so. ⁹ And I say to you, whoever divorces his wife, except for sexual immorality, and marries another, commits adultery; and whoever marries her who is divorced commits adultery."

¹⁰ His disciples said to Him, "If such is the case of the man with *his* wife, it is better not to marry."

¹¹ But He said to them, "**ALL CANNOT ACCEPT THIS SAYING, BUT ONLY *THOSE* TO WHOM IT HAS BEEN GIVEN:** ¹² **FOR THERE ARE EUNUCHS WHO WERE BORN THUS FROM *THEIR* MOTHER'S WOMB,** and there are eunuchs who were made eunuchs by men, and there are **EUNUCHS WHO HAVE MADE THEMSELVES EUNUCHS FOR THE KINGDOM OF HEAVEN'S SAKE**. He who is able to accept *it,* let him accept *it.*"

In describing the marriage relationship between men and women, Jesus says not all can accept this kind of relationship. This is because they are EUNUCHS. As the term is applied in Scripture by Jesus does not exclusively mean a castrated male. It cannot. First, Jesus says some were born that way – born in such a way that heterosexual marriage is out of the question. They were born that way. Then there are other conditions He mentions that reveal other people who cannot get married heterosexually. One of them are people who have made themselves Eunuchs FOR THE KINGDOM OF HEAVEN'S SAKE. This cannot be a castrated male. No one is required to cut off body parts or to mutilate themselves for the Kingdom of God. To go to Heaven, you do not need to chop off an arm or a leg or a sexual organ. You merely have to believe in Jesus.

Again, we look at **John 3:16**

16 For God so loved the world that He gave His only begotten Son, that **WHOEVER** believes in Him should not perish but have ever-lasting life.

And **Romans 10: 8-12**

8 But what does it say? "The word is near you, in your mouth and in your heart" (that is, the word of faith which we preach): 9 that if you confess with your mouth the Lord Jesus and believe in your heart that God has raised Him from the dead, you will be saved. 10 For with the heart one believes unto righteousness, and with the mouth confession is made unto salvation. 11 For the Scripture says, "**WHOEVER believes** on Him will not be put to shame." 12 For there is no distinction between Jew and Greek, for the same Lord over all is rich to all who call upon Him. 13 For "**WHOEVER** calls on the name of the Lord shall be saved."

Once we understand that **Eunuchs are people**, Biblically, who encompass a wide range of folks, but especially those who will not be married to the opposite sex, we see another Scripture that encompasses these Eunuchs.

***

Isaiah 56: 1-8

[3] Do not let the son of the foreigner who has joined himself to the Lord speak, **saying, "The Lord has utterly separated me from His people";** NOR LET THE EUNUCH SAY, "HERE I AM, A DRY TREE." [4] For thus says the **Lord: "To the eunuchs who keep My Sabbaths, And choose what pleases Me,   And hold fast My covenant,** [5] Even to them **I WILL GIVE IN MY** HOUSE and within My walls **A PLACE AND A NAME BETTER THAN THAT OF SONS AND DAUGHTERS;** I will give them **an everlasting name that shall not be cut off.**

[6] "Also the sons of the foreigner who join themselves to the Lord, to serve Him, and to love the name of the Lord, to be His servants—Everyone who keeps from defiling the Sabbath and holds fast My covenant— [7] Even them I will bring to My holy mountain, **and make them joyful in My house of** prayer. Their burnt offerings and their sacrifices *Will be* accepted on My altar; **For My house shall be called a house of prayer for all nations."** [8] **The Lord God, who gathers the outcasts** of Israel, says, "Yet I will gather to him *others* **besides those who are gathered to him."**

A Promise to Eunuchs

In the Old Testament law, Eunuchs were not allowed to participate as priests in the Temple. As a result of this exclusion, they could easily say or feel that spiritually they were a dry tree. This is true for gay folks in the modern era. Churches automatically exclude LGBT(+) people from ministry. Though this is changing and has changed considerably since the first openly gay affirming church in 1968, yet there are many churches who will not tolerate any such person among their priest-hood or clergy. Even in some nations it is still illegal to be in a same sex relationship. Moses gave the Law, prohibiting not only Eunuchs but people with eye problems, people with a hunchback, or any other physical deformity from serving at the Temple. But centuries later, Isaiah brings about a prophecy that is a game changer. Even so, the promise to the Eunuch, that God would give them a place within God's house had never been seen until that door opened in 1968. Since that time, Eunuch affirming churches and organizations have sprung up so fast that it is daunting to try keep track of them all.

The *history* of this movement is documented more fully in another book *The Holy Spirit and the Gay Community, The Early Years.* [11]

Many heterosexuals have become aware of and allied with this move of the Holy Spirit as well. For them, frequently the Scripture God has used is the episode in **Acts chapter ten**, where the Apostle Peter is given a vision of all the foods not Kosher to eat. God tells him to rise, kill and eat. He refuses, since he doesn't want to disobey the Jewish law. God then says that what God has cleansed to not call unclean. Next God tells him to accompany some gentiles that He has sent. He does and enters the home of a Roman Centurian named Cornelius.

---

11. Kader, Rev. Samuel, *The Holy Spirit and the Gay Community, The Early Years* SK Ministry Inc, 2022

By Jewish law, it was unlawful for Peter to enter their home, much less eat with them. But an angelic encounter prompted Cornelius to beckon Peter to come. As Peter begins to preach, his sermon is not even completed before the Holy Spirit falls upon all these outsiders, these Gentiles, and they are filled with the Holy Spirit and speak in tongues. Peter realizes that what God has cleansed (these Gentiles) he should not call unclean. So, he calls for them to baptized in water.

Our heterosexual allies have come to the same conclusion. God is powerfully moving by His Holy Spirit among the gay community, raising up LGBT (+) leaders and churches with an affirming, life giving message. These allies also see what Peter saw: that what God has cleansed do not call unclean.

So, those who fight this affirming LGBT (+) movement are on the wrong side of history and are unknowingly fighting God.

Chapter Eleven

A name better than sons and daughters.

According to **Isaiah 56**, there is a promise to the Eunuchs of the Kingdom of God. And according to Jesus in **Matthew 19: 12,**
¹² For there are eunuchs who were born thus from *their* mother's womb, and there are eunuchs who were made eunuchs by men, and there are eunuchs who have made themselves eunuchs for the kingdom of heaven's sake. He who is able to accept *it,* let him accept *it.* "

As we saw in the previous chapter, Eunuchs are not just men who've been castrated. He defines eunuchs as people who are not getting heterosexually married to an opposite sex partner, for several reasons. One such reason is that they have been born that way. They have been born without a heterosexual orientation. They might be gay, they might be asexual, or for other reasons of which they were born.

Nonetheless, they do not have an inclination to have a sexual partner of the opposite gender. They were born that way. Then there are also some who have made themselves eunuchs for the sake of the Kingdom of God. This is the proof that eunuchs are not just castrated men. No one has ever been required to castrate their genitals in order to get into Heaven. No one. The requirement to go to Heaven is to believe in Jesus as Lord, to believe God raised Him from the dead and to confess this as your testimony. (Romans 10:9-10). No where does God require body parts to be cut off in order to get into Heaven. So, those who have made themselves eunuchs for the sake of the Kingdom of God would be those, like the Apostle Paul, who chose to not get married in order to devote all their life and attention to serving God. Paul could not have fulfilled his ministry if he had a wife and children to take care of as well.

So, to this group of non-heterosexually married eunuchs, God made a promise:

Isaiah 56: 4-5 states

For thus says the Lord: "To the eunuchs who keep My Sabbaths,

And choose what pleases Me, And hold fast My covenant,

[5] Even to them I will give in My house, And within My walls a place and a name

Better than that of sons and daughters;

I will give them an everlasting name That shall not be cut off.

Eunuchs were given a name better than the rest of the church –who are the sons and daughters. To see this new name or new anointing and calling we look at Eunuchs in Scripture.

Scripturally, Eunuchs play a huge role in preparing the end time church for the return of Jesus.

Look at the following Scriptures:

2 Kings 9:30-35

[30] Now when Jehu had come to Jezreel, Jezebel heard *of it;* and she put paint on her eyes and adorned her head and looked through a window. [31] Then, as Jehu entered at the gate, she said, "*Is it* peace, Zimri, murderer of your master?"

[32] And he looked up at the window, and said, "Who *is* on my side? Who?" So **two** *or* **three EUNUCHS looked out at him.** [33] Then he said, "**Throw her down.**" So they threw her down, and *some* of her blood spattered on the wall and on the horses; and he trampled her underfoot. [34] And when he had gone in, he ate and drank. Then he said, "Go now, see to this accursed *woman,* and bury her, for she was a king's daughter." [35] So they went to bury her, but they found no more of her than the skull and the feet and the palms of *her* hands.

Revelation 2:18-23

[18] "And to the angel of the church in Thyatira write,

'These things says the Son of God, who has eyes like a flame of fire, and His feet like fine brass: [19] "I know your works, love, service, faith, and your patience; and *as* for your works, the last *are* more than the first. [20] Nevertheless I have a few things against you, because YOU ALLOW that woman Jezebel, who calls herself a prophetess, to TEACH AND SEDUCE MY SERVANTS to commit sexual immorality and eat things sacrificed to idols. (*politics as their god, Money as their god*) [21] And I gave her time to repent of her sexual immorality, and she did not repent. [22] Indeed I will cast her into a sickbed, and those who commit adultery with her into great tribulation, unless they repent of their deeds. [23] I will kill her children with death, and all the churches shall know that I am He who searches the minds and hearts. And I will give to each one of you according to your works.

Esther 2:12-15

[12] Each young woman's turn came to go in to King Ahasuerus after she had completed twelve months' preparation, according to the regulations for the women, for thus were the days of their preparation apportioned: six months with oil of myrrh, and six months with perfumes and preparations for beautifying women. [13] Thus *prepared, each* young woman went to the king, and she was given whatever she desired to take with her from the women's quarters to the king's palace. [14] In the evening she went, and in the morning she returned to the second house of the women, to the custody of Shaashgaz, the king's eunuch who kept the concubines. She would not go in to the king again unless the king delighted in her and called for her by name.

[15] Now when the turn came for Esther the daughter of Abihail the uncle of Mordecai, who had taken her as his daughter, to go in to the king, SHE REQUESTED NOTHING BUT WHAT HEGAI THE KING'S EUNUCH, the custodian of the women, ADVISED. And Esther obtained favor in the sight of all who saw her.

There are two wicked women called Jezebel in the Bible. One is a wicked Queen in Ancient Israel, the second is a false teacher in the New Testament church of Thyatira. But as we have already seen, we do not fight against flesh and blood, or people, but against powers and principalities. So though the ancient Queen Jezebel is long dead, the evil spirit that ruled her soul still exists, and showed up again in Thyatira. This evil spirit, based on the characteristics of these two individuals, hates the prophetic voice (threatened to kill Elijah), manipulates the throne, or the point person in power; while acting behind the scenes (she wrote letters in the name of her husband, King Ahab to have her neighbor killed). So, in a church, she would try to manipulate the Senior leadership by intimidation and control. In the New Testament we see her teaching people to be sexually immoral, to follow after worldly power rather than Jesus [eat things sacrificed to idols. (*politics as their god, money as their god*)]. This evil spirit tries to get the church off its game, and to take a detour from following the Holy Spirit. Now, we'll see how the Eunuch anointing has been reserved for these last days to prepare the church for the return of Christ.

In **2 Kings 9:30-35** it was the Eunuch who threw down the manipulating, controlling Jezebel. This ushered in a new move of God as her reign and control over the church (Israel) ended. No one else had the calling to be in the right place at the right time to throw down Jezebel. That same spirit which tries to trap and manipulate and control ministry gets thrown down by God's Eunuchs. Since the same spirit shows up again in the New Testament church of Thyatira, then it is also the Eunuchs who remove her influence from the church's worldly affair with other idols and sexual immorality. It is Eunuchs who will call the church back into sexual purity, and to stop being an adulteress with the world system.

Ephesians 5 [25-27]

Husbands, love your wives, just as Christ also loved the church and gave Himself for her, [26] that He might sanctify and cleanse her with the washing of water by the word, [27] that He might present her to Himself a glorious church, not having spot or wrinkle or any such thing, but that she should be holy and without blemish.

Esther 2:15

15 Now when the turn came for Esther the daughter of Abihail the uncle of Mordecai, who had taken her as his daughter, to go in to the king, she requested nothing but what Hegai the king's eunuch, the custodian of the women, advised.

Jesus is coming back for a Bride without spot of wrinkle.

Esther represents that Bride as she got ready to meet her King. When her time came to meet the King, she only took with her what the Eunuch Hegai advised her. I can picture him fixing her hair, tucking in her dress here and there, puffing out her sleeves, just so, he was the one who got her ready. The Eunuch did that.

THE EUNUCH GOT ESTHER READY FOR THE BRIDEGROOM

THE EUNUCH PREPARED ESTHER. HE GOT THE BRIDE READY TO MEET HER KING. EUNUCHS WILL PREPARE THE BRIDE TO BE WITHOUT SPOT OR WRINKLE TO MEET KING JESUS.

In the meantime, Eunuchs aren't welcome in so many segments of the church world. Yet the LGBT (+) eunuchs love Jesus and want to, and do, worship Him even without the church's permission.

Luke 15:15, 16

Then he went and joined himself to a citizen of that country, and he sent him into his fields to feed swine. And he would gladly have filled his stomach with the pods that the swine ate, **and no one gave him anything**.

In so many localities when a gay person tries to go to church and be involved, no one gives them anything. But gay folks, the Eunuchs are resourceful. They've had to be to survive. So, in Ft. Lauderdale,

Florida, for instance, when Eunuchs aren't welcome, they have church (worship) where they are.

In one gay bar in Ft. Lauderdale, Drag Queens take the last Sunday night a month to lip sync to worship songs and hymns. **It is the most popular night of the month in Ft. Lauderdale.** The world thinks Drag Queens, are just barflies. Like the Prodigal son of Luke 15, n**o one was giving them anything.**

So, the Father is finding them anyway, even in the bar!

The Drag Queens are not singing, but Lip syncing, which shows that sometimes you don't need to say anything to minister!

***

1977 KANSAS CITY PROPHECY

at the 50,000 people gathering Charismatic Conference

Jesus said:

"And other sheep I have which are not of this fold; them also I must bring, and they will hear My voice; and there will be one flock and one shepherd John 10:16 . (New King James)

This is further stated in the New Testament in **Ephesians 2:13-22**

13. But now in Christ Jesus you who once were far off have been made near by the blood of Christ. 14. For He Himself is our peace, who has made both one, and has broken down the middle wall of division between us, 15. having abolished in His flesh the enmity, that is, the law of commandments contained in ordinances, so as to

create in Himself one new man from the two, thus making peace, 16. and that He might reconcile them both to God in one body through the cross, thereby putting to death the enmity. 17. And He came and preached peace to you who were afar off and to those who were near.18. For through Him we both have access by one Spirit to the Father. 19. Now, therefore, you are no longer strangers and foreigners, but fellow citizens with the saints and members of the household of God, 20. having been built on the foundation of the apostles and prophets, Jesus Christ Himself being the chief cornerstone, 21. in whom the whole building, being joined together, grows into a holy temple in the Lord, 22. in whom you also are being built together for a habitation of God in the Spirit.

Initially, Scripture was referring to Jews and Gentiles coming together as one Body. But as time has gone on, Jesus clearly showed that He still had others that He was adding to His Body. Finally in 1968, another group, who were foreigners and strangers to the fellowship of Christian believers were added. Jesus Himself made both one and broke down the middle wall of division between us. This happened at Calvary at the Cross of Jesus. However, it has taken centuries for this truth to come to light.

When the Charismatic movement began in the late 1960's and early 1970's Charismatic gatherings began to surface in the largest stadiums in America. One pinnacle gathering took place at the Arrowhead Stadium in Kansas City in July 1977. Over 50,000 Charismatics Christians gathered together under the various banners and streams of that flow. Messianic Jews worshipped alongside Roman Catholics, and Assembly of God leadership. All streams were present as far *as the organizers knew*. Yet, the most remarkable thing that happened in the midst of this flow of worship, was a prophecy that came forth "**to mourn...weep...for the broken body of My son**."

"The Body of My Son is broken... mourn and weep, for the Body of My Son is broken...I am going to restore My people and reunite them. I am going to restore My people to the Glory that is Mine, so that the world might know that I am God and King and that I have come to redeem and save this earth..."[1]

The organizers of the conference felt that meant to have an even bigger conference with more people invited. So, the next year a conference was held in New York City with 100,000 people in attendance.[2]

God was clearly grieved that His Son's body was not together but broken. By this time the Jesus movement had been incorporated and accepted into the Charismatic movement, but gay Christians were neither acknowledged, nor received but were still demonized as heretics. The New York conference did not bring any further healing or wholeness to the body than they had in Kansas City. Gays were still outsiders.

Even churches who love their gay members were made outsiders.

On May 5, 2003, Ken Garfield, Religion Editor of the Charlotte Observer reported in an ongoing story that **McGill Baptist Church** was kicked out of the Cabarrus Baptist Association because they baptized two gay men. McGill, a century-old Concord, North Carolina church of 800 members was notified that the Cabarrus association of 81 Southern Baptist churches voted overwhelmingly to sever their ties with McGill. The two baptized gay men had been same sex partners

---

1. Stanley Burgess and Gary B. McGee, Editors, Dictionary of Pentecostal and Charismatic Movements, Grand Rapids, MI, Zondervan Publishing House, 1988, p. 139

2. Ibid

for six years and found God's love in that church. But the Southern Baptist Association found no love for the men or the church that baptized them.

The Rev. Randy Wadford, the association's missions director, read a statement after the vote in which he said "the homosexual lifestyle is contrary to God's will and plan for mankind. ... To allow individuals into the membership of a local church without evidence or testimony of true repentance is to condone the old lifestyle." Garfield reported. [3]

Garfield also reported that "while believing in the Christian tenet that all are sinners in need of God's forgiveness, the gay couple from McGill doesn't believe their relationship makes them sinners".

Why wouldn't these gay men think their relationship is sinful? Because God has been moving in the hearts and minds of His children to reveal His heart on the matter. Though the Cabarrus Baptist Association believed the men are still sinning just because they are still loving, it is their faulty interpretation of scripture that leads them and many others to this conclusion. But God knows how to work in the human heart to convince us of wrong doing. These believers have no twinge in their consciences that the love and home they share is a sin.

***

Evangelical Author Tony Campolo told a powerful story at a talk at North Park College Chapel on February 29, 1996.

---

3. http://www.charlotte.com/mld/observer/news/local/5787403. htm (last accessed June 24, 2005)

...Let me tell you one more story. I have a friend. He pastored a church up in Brooklyn. It was a dying community, a place where everything was disintegrating. He kept himself fed and clothes and his family cared for by, by doing odd jobs, one of which was doing funerals for the local undertaker when nobody else would take them. The man was a saint and he didn't know it so I would call him and get great stories because he never used them. And I would always say, Jim, anything good happen that I can tell, any good story that, anything happen this week?

He'd always say no.

"What about Tuesday at 11 o'clock? What were you doing then?" "Oh, he said, that was fascinating. The undertaker called me early in the morning because he had a man to bury who had died of AIDS and nobody wanted to take the funeral so I ended up taking the funeral."

I said, "What was it like?

He said, "About 25 homosexual men came and sat there. Never once, Tony, did they ever look up at me. The whole time I spoke their heads were down and they were looking at the floor. Never once did they ever make eye contact with me all during the funeral. We went out and got in some cars and we followed the hearse out to the cemetery, lowered the body into the grave. I stood on one side of the grave. These 25 some homosexual men on the other side. Standing there like statues, neither looking to the right or to the left, looking straight out into infinity. Never budging just sitting there, standing there rigid like statues. I read some scripture. I said some prayers. I committed the body to the grave. I said the benediction and I started to move - walk away, but they didn't move. They stood there as though frozen so I, I came back and I said, 'Excuse me, is there anything else I can do?'

"And one of the men said, 'Yes. I never go to church. Used to go to church but I don't go to church. The only thing I really liked about church was when they read from the Bible, especially the King James. I like the King James. You didn't read the 23rd psalm. I thought they always read that at funerals. Could you read the 23rd Psalm?'"

Jim opened the Bible and read the 23rd Psalm. Another man said, "There's a passage in the 3rd chapter of John about being born again. I like that passage."

John read that. Then a third man said, "The 8th chapter of Romans, right at the end, that's what keeps me going."

And Jim read to these homosexual men. "Neither height nor depth, neither principalities nor powers, neither things present, nor things to come, nothing, nothing can separate us from the love of God which is in Christ Jesus our Lord."

Nothing. And when he told me that, I hurt, I hurt, because I knew that these men wanted to hear the Bible but would never step foot inside a church because they are convinced that church people despise them. And do you know why they think church people despise them?

Because church people despise them. [4]

***

---

4. http://www.bridges-across.org/ba/campolo.htm (last accessed January 19, 2007)

BENNY HINN PROPHECY

Evangelist Benny Hinn was on the *Praise The Lord Program* on February 28, 1989, being interviewed by founder and host Paul Crouch. My co-pastor was watching the program live at 11 pm and the next morning called to see if I had seen the program. I hadn't but he invited me over to his house to watch the re-broadcast at 5 pm that next day. This time he had a tape recorder handy to capture the entire program. Once we heard this prophecy, my co-pastor, Bill Roberts, typed up the transcript and we mailed a copy to Benny Hinn. We got a nice letter from his secretary, thanking us for the transcript. Nobody denied that Hinn had said this about the gay community. The transcript is as follows:

2/28/89 GIVEN ON TRINITY BROADCASTING LIVE [TBN] 11 pm. EST

Paul Crouch had asked Benny Hinn if he had any word of prophecy from the Lord. He said he had and began to expound on the vision he had.

BENNY HINN: "I saw a tidal wave, I actually was taken into space in the Spirit and I saw a tidal wave coming towards our planet. I saw it splashing everywhere, every continent was splashed.

Then I saw myself and my pastors speaking against devils and when I spoke water flowed out of my mouth. Just like this. [Gesture]

So I asked the Lord "Lord, how will this happen?"

And the Lord spoke this to me; He said, "it is not going to happen in the large churches of America. It's not going to begin in the large churches of America, but it will begin in the living rooms of My people."

No charismatic movement has begun in the big denominations. It begins in small groups, then spreads. It took most of us people to catch up with the Charismatic Movement, 5, 6 years, 7 years later. The movement began in '67 with two Catholic priests at Notre Dame. But most guys like myself and many others were caught in '70-'72. I don't believe this move will take that long before really catches everybody.

The Lord told me, my ears heard my mouth talk; God said, "3½ months."

The latter part of May of this year, it will begin. It's not going to hit everyone at that time, but the move will begin in 3 ½ months.

PAUL CROUCH: "Could this be the beginning of that latter rain that we have been taught about?"

BENNY HINN: "It could be, because Smith Wigglesworth prophesied; Smith Wigglesworth was a man of God, he said the '80's, he actually said!

He said we would see a move of the Spirit first, which would be followed by a move of the Word. That has happened; we had the Charismatic Movement and the Word movement. He said at the end of the Word movement, just when the Word Movement would be closing up or changing, will come a move of God with a combination of both Spirit and Word which will bring the greatest move of God ever."

PAUL CROUCH: "How do you think that will really manifest itself?"

BENNY HINN: "Well I can tell you the way I believe, now again the Lord has not shown me details except to tell me it's going to begin in living rooms and God should..."

Well, I'm not really sure I like to tell you about it but I will.

The Lord said to me, He said, **"In that move I will save and deliver the people you consider to be a plague."** To me, **personally**.

PAUL CROUCH: **"And who might that be?"**

BENNY HINN: **"The homosexuals**. I said to the Lord, 'But Lord you can't do that!'"

"You know what the Lord said to me? God actually spoke these words to me.

'**The last move, the plague were the hippies**. And I brought them into the house of the Lord. **Now, the plague now is the homosexuals, and nobody wants to touch them."**

"But God Almighty is going to prove to the World and to the Church that He can clean them up!

It took a lot for me as a pastor recently in prayer to raise my hands and say 'Lord, bring them in!' You know as a pastor it's very easy to say I'm comfortable with what I've got. I don't want any group coming in here. I don't want any plagued people coming in here.

But the Lord said to me 'Do you believe I can do it?'"

"Yes!"

Benny Hinn. said that the next great move of God was going to be with homosexuals. He said he personally didn't want anything to do with that. But when God told Hinn that He was going to prove to the world and the church that He could clean us up, and further asked if Hinn believed that God could do this, he had to surrender and say "yes".

Now this was a shocking revelation to this television audience at the time. They sat there stunned. But after a long pause, once they translated this information through the filter of their old wine skin, they assumed what God meant by cleaning up the gays was they'd become heterosexuals.

But God did no such thing. Instead, without the permission or help from the church, God began to woo gay people out of night clubs and into His house of worship. Churches which were open and affirming and loved LGBT (+) people into the loving arms of Jesus sprang up almost overnight. When Hinn saw this tidal wave that would usher in this great revival it hit every single continent. Now if God wanted to bring in a global revival, there is one group of people that are already in place on every continent, in every nation, in every major city on Earth; that would be gay folks. That is who Hinn saw God using, much to his chagrin.

Additionally, in Hinn's vision he noted that God would prove to the world and to the church that He could clean them up. How is anyone spiritually made clean? By accepting Jesus Christ as Lord and Savior and recognizing the redeeming Blood of the Cross. Jesus has been doing exactly that, and without the former move of God helping God out. This has been a sovereign move of the Holy Spirit hovering over the dark and void places where gay folks assembled and by bringing light, life and love. It's real. On several occasions when heterosexual Christians came to see what this was all about, they recognize this is the same Holy Spirit at work that had once wooed them into the Kingdom of God.

1 Corinthians 12:21

21 And the eye cannot say to the hand, "I have no need of you."

Even though heterosexual Christians may declare that gays are now and forever an abomination and unredeemable, God still makes them part of His House of Prayer for All people. As a result, until the rest of the Body recognizes that they have LGBT (+) sisters and brothers, they remain crippled.

THEY NEED US:

It's the hand that cleans up the face. As the eye says to the hand, I don't need you, yet, when something gets in the eye that needs wiped away, how is this done without the hand? Or how are tears wiped away from the face when the soul is brokenhearted? The eye DOES need the hand

Enterprise church picnic w/ Sue and Tammy:

in the little town of Enterprise, Pennsylvania, there is a small church called Enterprise Bible Church. Now it just so happens that my spouse, Jerry Wright and I would attend it when we go on vacation to the area. It was a family church for Jerry when he was growing up and several of the members are relatives. This is a conservative area of the country, and the first few times I attended with my husband, I wasn't sure if I'd be welcomed or shunned. They accepted Jerry since he was a cousin to many of them and they all grew up together. Though I was initially guarded, I found that this little church in the woods still loved on us and often asked about us, sent us birthday cards, and welcomed us.

One lovely summer day Enterprise Bible Church was having a church picnic. Jerry and I sat at a picnic table with some of his cousins. But once they got up to mingle further, two church ladies, both moms, Tammy and also Sue, asked if they could sit with us and ask us a question. Tammy and Sue each had a child who was gay. They asked, "Is my child going to hell?"

Sue has a lesbian daughter who lives in Washington D.C., and Tammy has a grown son who is a gay man. We had a long discussion about what God is doing and has been doing for decades already. I finally also referred them to my first book, *"Openly Gay Openly Christian, How the Bible Really is Gay Friendly"*[5]

The former move of God, as they continue to fight what God is really doing, had brought torment to these moms. As we shared with them, Tammy and Sue finally had peace.

Eunuchs in Isaiah 56 have a promise.   **If they keep his covenant.** "For thus says the Lord: "To the eunuchs who keep My Sabbaths, and **choose what pleases Me, and hold fast My covenant, Even to them I will give in My house and within My walls a place and a name Better than that of sons and daughters; I will give them an everlasting name That shall not be cut off.**"

Our covenant is a blood covenant through the Cross of Jesus Christ. Our promise is eternal life and a life with the Holy Spirit.

---

5. Kader, Samuel *"Openly Gay Openly Christian, How the Bible Really is Gay Friendly"*, third edition 2024, SK Ministry.

Chapter Twelve

The Conflict Today

In each former move, the assumption is made that their historical move is the final word and ultimate truth and revelation from scripture. Then God comes along and shows the church that He has greater revelation and understanding. Consider the issue of slavery in the United States. Those who insisted that slavery was Scriptural and stood fast in that understanding, had to split from those who believed all men are created equal and thus slavery was morally wrong. This tore the Baptist churches into two factions, the Southern Baptists and the American Baptists. The issue of slavery not only tore churches apart, but brought about the Civil war, tearing the nation apart.

Once the Civil war ended it took the Southern Baptist Convention 150 years to apologize for their racist stand on slavery. It wasn't until 1995, that the Southern Baptist officials formally renounced the church's support of slavery and segregation.[1]

So, it is no historical surprise that when God does a new thing, bringing in more of His "others", that the staid church world denies what God is doing. It is even found fighting against God.

In over fifty years, since God raised up His point person, Rev. Troy D. Perry in October 1968, the church world has been continually fighting God's current move among the LGBT (+) community.

In my other book, *The Holy Spirit and the Gay Community, the Early Years*, I detail how many movers and shakers God actually used from the LGBT (+) community. God saved and raised up leaders in this current move of God. And just as Martin Luther had a verse that revealed that God wanted to restore salvation by faith alone; the overarching scripture for such a time as this is **John 3:16.** God so loves the world that **WHOEVER believes** in Him will not perish but have everlasting life. Whoever does not mean heterosexual people exclusively. it means *whoever believes, period*. Nonetheless, the former move of God within the church does not believe God. So, over the last 50 (+) years they continue to fight what God is doing among the Eunuch community. They use legislation, scare tactics, misinformation and outright lies. Some of the more notorious conflicts follow.

***

Anita Bryant

Anita Bryant (March 25, 1940 – December 16, 2024) was an American singer and a Christian activist. From 1977 to 1980, Bryant was an outspoken opponent of gay rights in the United States. In 1977, she founded the *Save Our Children* [2] campaign whose purpose was to repeal a local ordinance in Miami-Dade County, Florida that banned discrimination in areas of housing, employment, and public accommodation based on sexual orientation. She used scare tactics to declare that gay schoolteachers were a danger to America's children. She emphatically asserted that such teachers would recruit innocent children into a homosexual lifestyle. This, she decried, was fact, since gays presumably could not reproduce, thus they needed to recruit children in order to promulgate their numbers. This scare tactic was effective in reversing the non-discrimination law in Miami-Dade. She became known as God's Mother for America, a title her Baptist pastor deemed fit her. This campaign gained national attention and was the catalyst for the Religious Right and Jerry Falwell's Moral Majority to launch into the national fray. Previously, the other Christian organizations that were trying to woo Christians into the Republican party through moral concerns, had only a lackluster response to matters about abortion as well as the IRS threats to the removal of tax exemption from Christian institutions. Demonizing gays however evoked a visceral reaction. it brought crowds to the Save Our Children rallies, and huge

---

2. Save Our Children was an activist organization founded by Bryant to repeal gay rights. https://en.wikipedia.org/wiki/Save _Our_Children

fundraising results were obtained appealing to this fear and hatred of gays.

After her win in Florida, another similar challenge arose in California. Republican Assemblyman John Briggs introduced Proposition 6, which was intended to prohibit gays, lesbians and anyone supporting civil rights for them from working in California public schools. Anita Bryant flew to California to support this amendment.

As Kathy Baldock reported, "Emotions in California escalated. A gay sheriff committed suicide when someone outed him. Robert Hillsborough, a gay gardener was stabbed to death by four attackers outside his Mission District apartment as they screamed "Faggot! Faggot! Faggot! Here's one for Anita!" [3]

Despite the homophobic rhetoric, the Briggs Initiative ultimately failed in California.

But even though Bryant successfully demonized gay folks, and fought gay rights, and subsequently won her battle in Florida, it was not the outcome she wanted.

Throughout the country, supporters of gay rights condemned Bryant for her campaign. Assisted by prominent figures in music, film, and television, they retaliated by boycotting the orange juice that she promoted. The campaign ended on June 7, 1977 with a 69% majority vote to repeal the ordinance (which Dade County restored in 1998). Though this was a victory for Bryant, her public image was irreparably damaged and she found herself blacklisted. Her contract with the Florida Citrus Commission was terminated

---

3. Baldock, Kathy, *Walking the Bridgeless Canyon, Repairing the Breach Between the Church and the LGBTQ Community*, Canyon Walker Press, 2014, page 135

three years later. This left her financially insolvent, and she filed for bankruptcy twice.[4]

On October 14, 1977, Bryant was hit with a pie thrown at her by Thom L. Higgins. Bryant was on television when this happened and she responded, "At least it's a fruit pie." She then began to pray for God to forgive him "for his deviant lifestyle" then she began crying, still on camera. Her husband , Bob Greene, then ran into the parking lot and threw a remaining pie into Higgins' face.

Anita Bryant's victory at the polls caused an immediate backlash. Around the nation gay bars and other supporters boycotted orange juice. You wouldn't be seen drinking that! With these cancellations, her career began to plummet. Then her marriage fell apart and in 1980 she divorced her husband, Bob Green. The unforgiving fundamentalist church world would not forgive her for divorce. More and more church events were cancelled. Her reputation plummeted from a wholesome Christian mother to a self-righteous bigot. The ordinance she had repealed in Florida was reinstated 30 years later on November 25, 2008, when the Miami-Dade Circuit Courts declared the discriminational law unconstitutional.

Then finally, in 2021, Bryant's granddaughter, Sarah Green, came out publicly as a lesbian by announcing her pending marriage to a woman. She stated, however, that she was having difficulty deciding whether she should invite her grandmother to the ceremony. [5]

---

4. Wikipedia: https://en.wikipedia.org/wiki/Anita_Bryant last accessed 2/28/2025

5. Kader, Rev. Samuel, *The Holy Spirit and the Gay Community, The Early Years,* published by SK Ministry Inc 2022, page 13

Way back on the hot June night in 1977 before the vote took place in Florida, I was a young Christian attending a newly formed affirming Eunuch friendly LGBT (+) Church. As the Miami Dade vote approached, we fasted and prayed. We asked God to intervene. Though the election gave victory to the fear mongering by 69-31% and became a catalyst for more anti-gay rhetoric on the national stage, yet over and over God kept showing us how much He loves us and how much He will protect us from those who would hurt us. This affirming move of God for WHOSOEVER keeps moving forward sovereignly by the mighty hand of God alone.

It does not turn out well for those who fight the new thing God is doing.

***

Jerry Falwell

Pastor Jerry Falwell, was a pastor and founder of Liberty Baptist College. He joined Anita Bryant in 1977 at some of her Save Our Children rallies. At one, he declared to those attending: "Gays would just as soon kill you as look at you!"[6]

---

6. Baldock, Kathy, *Walking the Bridgeless Canyon, Repairing the Breach between the Church and the LGBTQ Community*, Canyon Walker Press, 2014, page 130

He transformed American politics by rallying the religious right into an electoral force, creating the *Moral Majority* in 1979.[7]

Falwell's empire brought in $200 million a year. His little country church grew to more than 24,000 members. Much of this on the backs of the gay folks he vilified.

Late in life he made a number of ludicrous comments, chief among them his claim that "the pagans, and the abortionists, and the feminists, and the gays and the lesbians who are actively trying to make that an alternative lifestyle, the ACLU, People for the American Way—all of them who have tried to secularize America" were in part responsible for the September 11, 2001 terrorist attacks. Falwell also said, as Timothy Noah notes, that "AIDS is the wrath of a just God against homosexuals." He claimed that feminists "just need a man in the house." He argued that evangelical environmental activism is the work of Satan.[8]

The **Rev. Jerry Sloan** died in November 2021. He was a gay pastor in the current move of God who also personally knew Jerry Falwell from Bible school where they both attended in the 1950's.

When Sloan came out in 1960, a pastor at his home church pulled him aside one day and told him he should leave and never come back. He later founded a Metropolitan Community Church in Des Moines, Iowa, and a local reporter covered the gay reverend at the new gay-friendly church. The article made its way back to his alma mater, and, as Sloan recalled, "They wrote me, demanding that I send

---

7. https://www.latimes.com/archives/la-xpm-2007-may-16-na-fal well16-story last accessed 2/28/2025

8. https://www.cbsnews.com/news/telling-the-story-of-jerry-falw ell/last accessed 2/28/2025

my diploma back to them. Not only that, but the vice president of the school, in a letter that he sent to me, closed it by saying 'we hope that you return to the faith, or God wipe your influence from the face of the earth.' Sloan saw the real potential for violence that lurked in Christian extremist circles. He spoke of "imprecatory prayers" — religious speech that invoked evil or curses on people. These words from the pulpit would inspire real violence, because believers might think to themselves, "Maybe God wants me to be the wielder of that two-by-four." He brought this up repeatedly over his life.[9]

Rev. Jerry Sloan had an obsession with far-right religious conservatives. He'd been a working minister himself, so he knew the Bible as well as any televangelist. After he moved to Sacramento in 1980, he formally devoted himself to tracking the radical religious right, and especially "The Old-Time Gospel Hour" which was Jerry Falwell's show. Falwell had raved about Sloan's mother's chocolate meringue pie when the two men were friends at the Missouri Baptist Bible College in 1950s. Launching his career as a pioneer of the Christian right, Falwell issued a "Declaration of War" on gay people. Later in the '80s, he asserted that gay people deserved to die of AIDS. [10] On this particular Sunday, Falwell said something that made Sloan especially angry. He went on a tirade against an LGBTQ-friendly church where Sloan had been a minister, **the Metropolitan Community Church**. He said: "*They are spoken of here in Jude as being brute beasts, that is, going to the baser lust of the flesh to live immorally.*

---

9. Gay Sacramento man won lawsuit against the Rev. Jerry Falwell | Sacramento Bee

10. "*Gay Sacramento man won lawsuit against the Rev. Jerry Falwell*" | Sacramento Bee

... Thank God, this vile and satanic system will one day be utterly annihilated and there will be celebration in heaven!" Sloan rushed out and bought a tape recorder to use for the rebroadcast — he wanted to keep a record of Falwell's smear against fellow Christians. And that impulse to document hatred allowed the enterprising Sacramento activist to win seed money for the city's first LGBTQ community center.

Although Sloan first made his mark by successfully suing Falwell over those comments in the '80s, he was an activist for decades, preaching that the machinations of Christian right called for constant vigilance. He co-founded Project Tocsin — named after an alarm bell — to monitor the far right. His skirmish with Falwell exemplified the kind of activism he loved: confrontational, demanding and grounded in truth.

Sloan also networked with other activists to bolster their work. "He helped me understand the importance of extremist political tactics in (the) Republican Party," said Hans Johnson, who was a young progressive organizer in D.C. when he was first introduced to Sloan. In the early '90s, Johnson said, "The religious right was increasingly obsessed with anti-LGBT appeals." Johnson eventually moved to Southern California and was able to visit Sacramento to see Sloan more often in person. Over the years, he came to see Sloan's point of view as more prescient than ever — particularly now, he said, as Republicans' obsession with LGBT people reaches new levels of hysteria, with anti-trans and now anti-drag queen legislation garnering support in conservative legislatures across the country.

Sloan was attuned to bigotry against LGBTQ people decades earlier. In 1984, Sloan hadn't recorded Falwell's comments with the intention of suing — he just wanted to track far-right attacks on gay people. But when the televangelist happened to come to Sacramento in July, a few months after the broadcast, Sloan decided to confront him during a taping of "*Look Who's Talking*" on Channel 3. Falwell had been his friend. During the 1955-1956 school year, Falwell and Sloan had driven from their college in Springfield, Missouri, to Sloan's hometown of Kansas City, Missouri, every weekend for work. Sloan's mother, Gloria, often made the young men a Sunday dinner.

So, he went to the live talk show's taping, and Falwell recognized him. And then, while the cameras were rolling and Sloan started to repeat Falwell's own words to him, **Falwell said, "That's an absolute lie, Jerry."** The Sacramento Bee reported at the time that **Falwell told him, "I'll threaten you. ... I'll give $5,000 — I'm saying this on TV — if you can produce that tape**." Sloan said sure, he had a tape. Later, he told The Bee, "The man called me a liar. ... I needed some personal vindication."

Sloan, of course, produced the tape, and **Falwell refused to pay him**. So, **Sloan sued Falwell, not for slandering gay people, but for lying**. With the help of Sacramento attorney Rosemary Metrailer — who initially took his case pro bono — Sloan won his breach of contract case. The judge ordered Falwell to pay up, and the Los Angeles Times ran the memorable headline "**Falwell Ordered to Pay $5,000 to Gay Who Met Evangelist's Challenge**." That triumphant gay told the paper, "I did it for the principle of the thing. ... His statements are dangerous to the gay and lesbian community. He has said disastrous things about various and sundry people, and he's always tried to squirm out of it."[11]

Falwell claimed in the paper that he was the victim of "harassment by a militant homosexual group in Sacramento" (the group

---

11. ibid

was apparently just Sloan and Metrailer, his lesbian attorney). As he promised, **Falwell appealed, and lost again on appeal.** Ultimately, his organization — the Moral Majority, a conservative political group that railed against women's rights, abortion rights and gay rights until dissolving in 1989 — **had to pay Sloan $8,982.90, the $5,000 plus interest, attorneys' fees and punitive damages for a suit the judges found "wholly frivolous and totally without merit."** As Metrailer told The Bee in 2014, **"We made him be accountable for the hatred he was espousing.** The case made international news." In an interview with CapRadio for StoryCorps, Metrailer and Sloan recalled that **Falwell attempted to impose a "no gloating" stipulation on the check.** He didn't want Sloan to call a news conference. Sloan told Metrailer at the time not to bother fighting Falwell's demand — **he'd just have his mother, Gloria, call a news conference for him**. Sloan had a giant blowup of the check made. After his final 1986 victory, he told the Los Angeles Times that Falwell "indicated that I was a liar and that I was not a reliable person," so the lawsuit "was a matter of personal integrity."

He gave much of the winnings to buy chairs, plants and ceiling fans for the Lambda Community Center, which has since changed its name to the Sacramento LGBT Community Center and provides services to LGBTQ Sacramentans to this day.

"You can say that Jerry Falwell was kind of a godfather of the community center in Sacramento," Sloan said in the StoryCorps interview. "We did dedicate a room there to him (Falwell). It was the toilet."

At the time of Jerry Falwell's death the LA times quoted Matt Foreman, executive director of the National Gay and Lesbian Task Force, as saying: "Unfortunately, we will always remember him as a founder and leader of America's anti-gay industry, someone who exacerbated the nation's appalling response to the onslaught of the

AIDS epidemic, someone who demonized and vilified us for political gain and someone who used religion to divide rather than unite our nation." [12]

At the time of his death, Falwell was working to revive the Moral Majority, which he disbanded in 1989 amid lackluster fundraising.[13]

***

Charisma Magazine

Though the Metropolitan Community Churches were the first fully affirming LGBT (+) churches around, it wasn't long before other groups began to form as well. Pentecostal, Charismatic, and Evangelical churches sprang up within the LGBT (+) community and many of them joined together in fellowship organizations. One of these newer churches was Potter's House in Tampa Florida, and the founding pastor was Robert Morgan. Potter's House Fellowship 5th Anniversary Weekend took place November 14-16, 2003, in Tampa, Florida. They were a part of the Reconciling Pentecostal International organization, so many of the churches from that group planned to attend. Also, because one of their guest speakers was none other than famous tele-

---

12. **Preacher built religious right into a political force**

13. https://www.latimes.com/archives/la-xpm-2007-may-16-na-fal well16-story.html

vision personality Tammy Faye Bakker, the television crews also came in force. Two other guest speakers were Bishop Carlton Pearson from Tulsa, Oklahoma, and Rev. D.E. Paulk of Atlanta, Georgia. These last two were recently preaching controversial theology, and they brought it to the pulpit in Tampa.   For this reason, that caused Rev. Morgan quite a bit of trouble. However, Tammy Faye Bakker preached a powerful message on forgiveness that caused even the camera crews to wipe tears away from their eyes. In the meantime, Charisma Magazine sent a "spy" to the anniversary and then reported on the event in a later edition.

***

In the April 2004 issue of Charisma Magazine, they reported that they had a "spy" at the Tampa meeting. From their web site they reported:

First Word Heretics Among Us
By J. Lee Grady

Last fall I was shocked to learn that a group of charismatic church leaders were convening in Tampa, Florida, to discuss ways they could promote a homosexual agenda. I thought only Episcopalians were sliding in this direction, so I sent an undercover reporter to the meeting. She sat in the back of the room and listened while these leaders suggested ways to spread their unorthodox message.

They met in a "gay-affirming" church led by a former Assemblies of God minister. Attendees included Oklahoma-based pastor Carlton Pearson, who made headlines last year when he announced that he had adopted a more "inclusive" theology. Pearson already believes everyone is saved, yet now he has stepped into deeper doctrinal quicksand with the idea that unrepentant homosexuals will get a free ticket to heaven.

Pearson said he hoped gay leaders would "build silent bridges" by joining the staffs of "heterosexual churches" and gradually convincing them to accept the gay lifestyle. Another pastor told the group: "We do not believe that loving someone of the same sex in a committed, monogamous relationship is a sin."

Did you ever imagine we would see a day when so-called Spirit-filled ministers would call for the open acceptance of sexual perversion? If you can't hear the alarm bell buzzing, please have your ears checked. We need to pull our heads out of the sand and recognize that the American church is racing toward the biggest culture clash of our time. [14]

Because Pearson had left traditional theology about salvation, and slipped into Universalism, (everyone is already saved no matter what they believe) Charisma magazine found that to be the more sensational story and useful to prove their theory that no one at the church anniversary could be anything but a heretic. But Pearson was responsible for his own ministry and theology. As he delved into this Universalism, he actually lost his mega church and credibility among his peers.

Pastor D.E. Paulk additionally left traditional Christianity as found in the Bible, where Jesus says He is the way, the truth and the Life. His church espouses a different gospel that says " we perceive Christ cannot be, and will not be, restricted to Christianity..." and "the work of the Holy Spirit is to lead us into ALL truth...not exclusively biblical or

14. http://www.charismamag.com/articledisplay.pl/?ArticleID=86 73

Christian truths... additionally their web site states that .."they believe that the Christ Spirit is present in all of creation and cannot be defined by, nor confined to, Christianity." [15]

But Robert Morgan, his church, and the other guests still were undisputed disciples and followers of Jesus Christ of Nazareth, the Savior of the World. They were standing firm on **John 3:16** that whoever believed in Jesus would not perish but have everlasting life. It seemed that both Pearson and Paulk became allies to the LGBTQ (+) community but had very divergent views from what God was doing in bringing gay folks to Himself through a born again experience, through the Cross of Calvary and the Blood of Jesus. Pastor Robert Morgan had not strayed from that truth but merely had invited those who were once from traditional Christianity and who had become allies to the community to come and speak. This was an unfortunate mistake. He told me that he was not aware that they were going to bring theology that contradicts the very essence of what Jesus accomplished on the Cross for those who would put their trust in Him alone.

The essence of what the LGBT (+) Christian movement believes is the same as the rest of the Christian world. Namely, both what **John 3:16** states and the succinct passage of **Romans 10:9-11**

9 that if you confess with your mouth the Lord Jesus and believe in your heart that God has raised Him from the dead, you will be saved. 10 For with the heart one believes unto righteousness,

---

15. D. E. Paulk is the Senior Pastor of Spirit and Truth Sanctuary in Atlanta, GA. His information can be found at the church web page, http://www.mytruthsanctuary.com/aboutus.html last accessed 3/10/2025

and with the mouth confession is made unto salvation. 11 For the Scripture says, "Whoever believes on Him will not be put to shame."

Though Charisma Magazine picked up on Carlton Pearsons' divergence from Christianity, they did not notice the move of the Holy Spirit nonetheless in that weekend. After Tammy Faye Bakker (Messner) had preached, several gay men got baptized in the hotel pool that evening. As of 2025, Charisma still continues to act as if it is impossible for a LGBT (+) person to be saved, be born again, be filled with the Holy Spirit, or to walk with God. They continue to be on the wrong side of history. Once again, the former move of God fights the current move of God.

***

Marsha Stevens

Marsha became a Christian as a sixteen-year-old high school student in 1969. Shortly after, she wrote the song "For Those Tears I Died (Come to the Water)" Her song eventually became widely known and sung by Christian youth groups and churches across the United States. Over time, it was included in Christian songbooks as well as church hymnals. It's hard to find a hymnal that doesn't include it.

As her popularity grew, Marsha became part of a group called *Children of the Day*, along with her sister Wendy Carter and friends Peter Jacobs and Russ Stevens. The group played regularly at their home church, Calvary Chapel[16] in Costa Mesa, California, where Chuck Smith was the pastor.

Because of the widespread distribution and success of *For Those Tears I Died*, Stevens received an entry in the *Encyclopedia of Contemporary Christian Music*. In it, her impact on the early Jesus Music scene is recognized, with Stevens being referred to as "**The Mother of Contemporary Christian Music**".[17]

She married band member Russ Stevens, and they remained married for seven years and had two children. After the divorce, Marsha became a Registered Nurse to support herself and her children. In 1981 she came out as a lesbian, and Russ Stevens would have nothing more to do with her.

Furthermore, after coming out publicly as a lesbian following her divorce, Stevens faced severe criticism from Christians, churches, and the Christian music industry. Her songs were torn from hymnals and songbooks with the torn pages sent to her in the mail. As with Lonnie Frisbee, who she personally knew, the anointing is recognized and celebrated as long as the church thinks you are following their rules instead of the leading of the Holy Spirit. Despite this acrimonious response from the Church, Marsha Steven's ministry flourishes. She ministers regularly among the LGBT (+) Christian community. She has written many more songs, recorded more albums and continues to travel to churches and church conferences to minister regularly. If God be for us, who can be against us.

---

16. https://en.m.wikipedia.org/wiki/Calvary_Chapel

17. https://en.m.wikipedia.org/wiki/Marsha_Stevens

***

Joy Metropolitan Community Church, Orlando, Florida

According to a television news report by Nick Papantonis, [18] of WFTV on March 13, 2025 at 8:33 pm EDT [19], A growing number of protesters have been interrupting Sunday worship services at progressive, affirming, Orange County churches in Orlando Florida. On March 9, 2025 a group of conservative Christians from a "Sanford-based church that, in its core beliefs, urges followers to preach the gospel, salvation, and traditional masculine values.[20] What started with a couple and a bullhorn on the sidewalk outside, has turned into a group of six or seven men, children in tow, entering the sanctuary and standing up to demonstrate midway

---

18. Nick Papantonis, of WFTV, journalist and TV personality in Orlando Florida.
    https://www.wftv.com/author/nick-papantonis/

19. https://www.wftv.com/news/local/church-worship-services-disrupted-by-protesters-prompting-security-concerns/XWFGYVO52VDKHOWIHJZ74D3J7U/

20. Ibid

through a sermon."[21] Several congregant members made videos of the vitriolic outburst, when the men began shouting that this was an abomination. Many of the congregants present posted the invasion of the worship service to social media, which went viral. The preacher then loudly led the congregation in a rousing hymn sing.

"Rev. Terri Steed Pierce's Joy Metropolitan Community Church in Orlando was targeted last Sunday, one of several hit that day.

"They were greeted. They were given welcome bags that have a little snack and some of the little tchotchkes in it," Steed Pierce said. "One of them was sitting in the back acting a little strange, and so that caught people's attention. But you just don't imagine this is going to happen."

Steed Pierce and other pastors said the group appears to be targeting churches that welcome LGBTQ community members or are led by female pastors."[22]

At least four churches in the Windermere and Orlando Florida areas have been targeted since November, 2024, with some churches hit with frequent demonstration occurrences.

Clearly the demonstrators felt they were helping God, by calling members of affirming congregations an abomination. But like so many times in the past, the former move of God finds itself fighting God, and is on the wrong side of history. Nonetheless, as God moves forward, He blesses His new wineskin with faith, hope, and more love.

---

21. Ibid

22. Ibid

Chapter Thirteen

The Cost to Follow Christ

On **January 21, 2025, as part of the inaugural services for President Donald Trump, a worship service was held in Washington D.C.**

During that service, at the Washington National Cathedral, Rev. Mariann Budde the Episcopal Bishop of Washington asked President Trump to show mercy to those Americans who were afraid. She referred specifically to gay, lesbian and transgender children, some of whom she said, "fear for their lives." it was a call for mercy, not even a call to change his political agenda. A day before Budde's sermon, Trump had capped off his first day in office by signing an executive order that said the federal government would recognize only two sexes, male and female. [1]

In Luke 4, Jesus said something similar to what Rev. Budde preached:

Luke 4:18

The Spirit of the LORD is upon Me, Because He has anointed Me
  To preach the gospel to the poor; He has sent Me to heal the
  brokenhearted, To proclaim liberty to the captives And recovery of
  sight to the blind, To set at liberty those who are oppressed.

The response to Bishop Budde's request for mercy was quick and vitriolic.

White House press secretary Karoline Leavitt on Wednesday also took
  aim at Budde in comments to Fox News, saying she had chosen
  to "weaponize the pulpit," adding that the bishop's remarks "were
  egregious, and she should apologize to President Trump for the lies
  that she told."

Asked Wednesday how she would respond to the vitriol she has received in the aftermath of her sermon, Budde said she was trying
  "to encourage a different kind of conversation."[2]

Franklin Graham, the famous evangelist and son of evangelist Billy
Graham, also was quick to respond. His comments show clearly how
the former move of God reacts to the concept of God moving among
the least of these.

Rev. Franklin Graham slammed Rt. Rev. Mariann Budde for a
  "sexual political agenda" after she pleaded with President Don-

---

1. Bishop Mariann Budde defends plea directed at Trump during
    inaugural prayer service Jan. 22, 2025, 11:01 PM EST

2. Ibid

ald Trump to "have mercy" on "immigrants and LGBTQ Americans."[3] "She is a socialist, activist, LGBTQ+ agenda, and that's, you know, so she's just wrong," he continued. "So these are activists, and no question, they hate Trump. I don't know why they hate Trump. Trump stands for truth."

He continued:

She's misleading people, and she was wrong, and I would hope that whoever the powers that be would put somebody in the cathedral who doesn't have a political agenda or a sexual political agenda, but just somebody who would be there to open up the word of God and to encourage people to worship God."[4][5]

This begs the question, what motivates the former move to so tenaciously hang onto the viewpoint they espouse.

New wine needs new wineskins as Jesus pointed out[6] If a person stays stuck and doesn't move forward, they fall behind when God is moving. Of course, the enemy of God is at work behind the scenes to keep God's House divided, but in addition we can see other things in operation.

---

3. https://www.rawstory.com/tag/lgbtq last accessed 3/12/2025

4. Ibid

5. https://baptistnews.com/article/franklin-graham-says-trump-stands-with-truth/
Article January 23, 2025 last accessed 1/25/2025

6. Matthew 9:17

Proverbs 29:25

The **fear of man** brings a snare, but whoever trusts in the Lord shall
be safe.

People will often operate in fear. They fear what others will say, think
or do if they support an unpopular construct.

NPR reported on a pastor who felt this was exactly the case.[7]

They reported a conversation with Russell Moore who was one of the
top officials in the Southern Baptist Convention.

> On why he thinks Christianity is in crisis:
>
> It was the result of having multiple pastors tell me, essentially, the
> same story about quoting the Sermon on the Mount, parentheti-
> cally, in their preaching — "turn the other cheek" — [and] to have
> someone come up after to say, "Where did you get those liberal talk-
> ing points?" And what was alarming to me is that in most of these
> scenarios, when the pastor would say, "I'm literally quoting Jesus
> Christ," the response would not be, "I apologize." The response
> would be, "Yes, but that doesn't work anymore. That's weak." And
> when we get to the point where the teachings of Jesus himself are
> seen as subversive to us, then we're in a crisis.

Russell further stated:

> I don't think we fix it by fighting a war for the soul of evangelicalism.
> I really don't think we can fix it at the movement level. And that's
> one of the reasons why, when I'm talking to Christians who are

---

7. https://www.npr.org/2023/08/08/1192663920/southern-bapt
ist-convention-donald-trump-christianity   last   accessed
3/12/2025

concerned about this, my counsel is always "small and local." I think we have to do something different and show a different way. And I see in history every time that something renewing and reviving has happened, it's happened that way. It's happened at a small level with people simply refusing to go with the stream of the church culture at the time.[8]

What does Scripture say about the widow, the orphan, the stranger, the alien.

"Do not oppress the widow or the fatherless, The alien or the poor. Let none of you plan evil in his heart Against his brother.'"Zecha riah 7:10 NKJV

Yet, the fear of others is not so new.

In John 20:19 the disciples of Jesus hid behind locked doors.

19 Then, the same day evening, being the first day of the week, when the doors were shut where the disciples were assembled, for FEAR OF THE JEWS, Jesus came and stood in the midst, and said to them, "Peace be with you.

They were afraid of the Jews, but *who were the disciples*? They were all Jewish. Thus, after the Crucifixion the disciples of Christ were afraid of their own relatives. They were afraid of their parents, their cousins, their brothers and sisters. It took a visitation from Jesus Himself to calm their fears.

Also, it was like Peter –because he feared what people would do, if they knew he was a Christ follower, thus he denied Jesus three times.

People also Fear that by standing with the truth, as God is revealing it, your income will be affected. MANY NON-AFFIRMING MINISTERS KNOW THE TRUTH, BUT WON'T SHARE IT.

---

8. Ibid

They know God has been moving among the Eunuch, LGBTQ (+) community, but refuse to admit it. So, for some it's all about the money.

Judas Iscariot had the anointing given to him by Jesus to heal the sick, cast out devils, and raise the dead. But he traded Christ for cash. Thirty pieces of silver, money, made a lousy god. The religious right, the Pharisees of our day have traded Christ for cash, and Providence for power, as they bedded with politics.

Then there's the FEAR that they would be put out of the synagogue (the Church). Many Church leaders, musicians who are gay, for instance, stay in the closet out of fear that they'll lose their position in the church or be ousted altogether. A lot of stress and energy goes into hiding truth in the closet.

Mark 7:9 "Jesus said to them, "All too well you **reject** the **commandment** of God, that you may keep your tradition. "

What is this Commandment? It is to love your neighbor.

> **What is this Commandment? It is to love your neighbor.**

The question then becomes is it love? Is our behavior or our attitude one of love?

God's new move will always involve love, because God is Love. Love your neighbor, feed hungry.

Matthew 25: 31-40

31 "When the Son of Man comes in His glory, and all the [c]holy angels with Him, then He will sit on the throne of His glory. 32 All the nations will be gathered before Him, and He will separate

them one from another, as a shepherd divides *his* sheep from the goats. **33** And He will set the sheep on His right hand, but the goats on the left. **34** Then the King will say to those on His right hand, 'Come, you blessed of My Father, inherit the kingdom prepared for you from the foundation of the world: **35** for I was hungry and you gave Me food; I was thirsty and you gave Me drink; I was a stranger and you took Me in; **36** I *was* naked and you clothed Me; I was sick and you visited Me; I was in prison and you came to Me.'

37 "Then the righteous will answer Him, saying, 'Lord, when did we see You hungry and feed *You,* or thirsty and give *You* drink? **38** When did we see You a stranger and take *You* in, or naked and clothe *You?* **39** Or when did we see You sick, or in prison, and come to You?' **40** And the King will answer and say to them, 'Assuredly, I say to you, inasmuch as you did *it* to one of the least of these My brethren, you did *it* to Me.'

How can we know if a current move is of God or misguided?

First of all, how are people treated? Is it with Love?

As we saw in **Acts 9:3-5**

3 As he journeyed he came near Damascus, and suddenly a light shone around him from heaven. **4** Then he fell to the ground, and heard a voice saying to him, "Saul, Saul, why are you persecuting Me?"

5 And he said, "Who are You, Lord?"

Then the Lord said, "I am Jesus, whom you are persecuting. It *is* hard for you to kick against the goads."

Saul of Tarsus was a Pharisee of Pharisees. He was an ardent Moses follower, and when Christ followers became prolific, he felt it was his duty to help God and to fight God's battle for Him. Yet, once Saul became a Christian during this Damascus road encounter, he realized he had it wrong. He did not need to fight God's people nor try to stop them.

The new way, the Scriptural way, was God's way, as Paul learned.

In **Romans 12: 14-21**, Paul wrote:

14 Bless those who persecute you; bless and do not curse. 15 Rejoice with those who rejoice, and weep with those who weep. 16 Be of the same mind toward one another. Do not set your mind on high things, but associate with the humble. Do not be wise in your own opinion.

17 Repay no one evil for evil. Have regard for good things in the sight of all men. 18 If it is possible, as much as depends on you, live peaceably with all men. 19 Beloved, do not avenge yourselves, but *rather* give place to wrath; for it is written, "Vengeance *is* Mine, I will repay," says the Lord. 20 Therefore

"If your enemy is hungry, feed him;

If he is thirsty, give him a drink;

For in so doing you will heap coals of fire on his head."

21 Do not be overcome by evil but overcome evil with good.

Vengeance is God's. He does not need us to fight his battles. So, if a new move surfaces on the horizon, or even if it is heresy, God is big enough to deal with it. His mandate to us is to feed the hungry enemy, to give a drink to a thirsty opponent. When the Church fights God, it will do the opposite. They'll go to court, they'll get laws passed to stop God's move from going forward. But how did Jesus respond when faced with His enemies as they dragged Him before Pilot to have Him killed? Did He argue with them, did He prove they were wrong, Did He strike them with lightning? What did He say, as they stood vehemently accusing Him? NOTHING. He didn't need to. He knew Who He was and is, He didn't have anything to prove. But when a former move of God is fighting God, they won't stop arguing. They'll get on talk shows, they'll write books to prove they're right. Nonetheless they are on the wrong side of history, and as Jesus said to Saul on the road to Damascus, "Why are you fighting Me?" Saul thought he was fighting Christians. Jesus took it personally and said, look buddy, you're fighting God. And it is dangerous, and it turns out badly to keep kicking against God's plan and purpose. No one is big enough to fight God and win. No one.

Consider what criteria Jesus will use when judgement day arrives: Matthew 25:31-40

31 "When the Son of Man comes in His glory, and all the holy angels with Him, then He will sit on the throne of His glory. **32** All the nations will be gathered before Him, and He will separate them one from another, as a shepherd divides *his* sheep from the goats. **33** And He will set the sheep on His right hand, but the goats on the left. **34** Then the King will say to those on His right hand, 'Come, you blessed of My Father, inherit the kingdom prepared for you from the foundation of the world: **35** for I was hungry and you gave Me food; I was thirsty and you gave Me drink; I was a stranger and you took Me in; **36** I *was* naked and you clothed Me; I was sick and you visited Me; I was in prison and you came to Me.'

37 "Then the righteous will answer Him, saying, 'Lord, when did we see You hungry and feed *You,* or thirsty and give *You* drink? **38** When did we see You a stranger and take *You* in, or naked and clothe *You?* **39** Or when did we see You sick, or in prison, and come to You?' **40** And the King will answer and say to them, 'Assuredly, I say to you, inasmuch as you did *it* to one of the least of these My brethren, **YOU DID IT TO ME**.'

Secondly, Jesus says we will know them by their fruits.

Matthew 7:15-20

15 "Beware of false prophets, who come to you in sheep's clothing, but inwardly they are ravenous wolves. **16** You will know them by their fruits. Do men gather grapes from thornbushes or figs from thistles? [17] Even so, every good tree bears good fruit, but a bad tree bears bad fruit. [18] A good tree cannot bear bad fruit, nor *can* a bad tree bear good fruit. [19] Every tree that does not bear good fruit is cut down and thrown into the fire. [20] Therefore by their fruits you will know them.

We'll know them by their fruits. We once had a pear tree. The wintertime brought forth no fruit. In the Spring, little white pear blossoms would appear. They were pretty and even had a slight fragrance; but it was still not yet fruit. Over the Summer the fruit would develop until it was ripe and luscious. So it is with people. It takes time for their character to develop into recognizable fruit.

The Fake Fruit cannot be maintained over the long-haul. We must look at long range picture to see fruit.

In **John 17: 20-23**, Jesus prayed His high priestly prayer for His people.

[20] "I do not pray for these alone, but also for those who will believe in Me through their word; [21] that they all may be one, as You, Father, *are* in Me, and I in You; that they also may be one in Us, that the world may believe that You sent Me. [22] And the glory which You gave Me I have given them, that they may be one just as We are one: [23] I in them, and You in Me; that they may be made perfect in one, and that the world may know that You have sent Me, and have loved them as You have loved Me.

What is at stake is that the world will recognize that God sent Jesus, not another or every other so-called Messiah. Jesus is **the** way, **the** truth and **the** life.

As **John 8:31-32** records

31 Then Jesus said to those Jews who believed Him, "If you abide in My word, you are My disciples indeed. **32** And you shall know the truth, and the truth shall make you free."

One has to abide in the Word to be current with God. Just as Martin Luther got a revelation from the Word, that the just shall live by faith, when God is doing a new thing, it will agree with the Word of God. So, each movement has a watchword that is a catalyst for what God is doing today. In the affirming movement we see the passages about Eunuchs, such as Matthew 19, Isaiah 56, and others as well as John 3:16 that Whosoever believes in Jesus will be saved. There is no exclusion policy that disqualifies whether or not someone is a whosoever, if they believe.

The Apostle John saw someone using the name of Jesus, doing miracles, yet this individual was not a part of the Jesus followers. We feel if they don't do it our way, if they aren't part of our group, if they have a different take on Jesus than what we were taught, they are wrong, and we must resist them. Stop them. Forbid them. Jesus disagrees.

Mark 9:38

38 Now John answered Him, saying, "Teacher, we saw someone who does not follow us casting out demons in Your name, and we forbade him because he does not follow us."

39 But Jesus said, "Do not forbid him, for no one who works a miracle in My name can soon afterward speak evil of Me. **40** For he who is not against us is on our side. **41** For whoever gives you a cup of water to drink in My name, because you belong to Christ, assuredly, I say to you, he will by no means lose his reward.

Matthew 25 – the Bridegroom cometh

A final consideration is found in **Matthew 25:1-10.** there are five foolish virgins and five wise ones. This parable is about the church in the final hour. It is *only* the church because all ten virgins are waiting for the Bridegroom. The world is not waiting for the Bridegroom Jesus to return, they don't even believe in Him. However, of the believers mentioned, five are foolish. They are not current with the Holy Spirit; their oil is running out. Oil is symbolic of both the presence of the Holy Spirit and the anointing. Theirs is running out. This is a former move of God. They once had oil, but didn't stay filled up, or current with what God is doing. At the moment the Bridegroom returns only those who are ready are admitted. Only those who are current are admitted when Jesus returns for His Bride who is without spot or wrinkle. Does this mean that former move of God believers don't go to Heaven. No, but just not right away.

In Revelation 13 the Antichrist comes on the scene.

⁵ And he was given a mouth speaking great things and blas-phemies, and he was given authority to continue for forty-two months. ⁶ Then he opened his mouth in blasphemy against God, to blaspheme His name, His tabernacle, and those who dwell in heav-en. ⁷ **It was granted to him to make war with the saints and to overcome them.** And authority was given him over every tribe, tongue, and nation. ⁸ All who dwell on the earth will worship him, **whose names have not been written in the Book of Life of the Lamb** slain from the foundation of the world.

Here are believers who are attacked by Satan's Antichrist. He institutes a world-wide economic system where all people are prohibited from buying or selling unless they take a physical demonic mark, which indicates they first bowed down to worship this antichrist. Those who won't, get beheaded, but they find their names written in Heaven, in the Lamb's book of Life, and they now have eternity with Christ Jesus.

These foolish virgins have trials and tribulations when once they are left behind. But they do know enough to not take the Antichrist's mark. They stay on the side of Christ, even to the death.

It is critical in these last days to stay current with God. Time is running out.

To discover whether or not a new move is actually of God, the advice Gamaliel gave the Sanhedrin still stands.

Act 5:38-39

[38] And now I say to you, keep away from these men and let them alone; for if this plan or this work is of men, it will come to nothing; [39] but if it is of God, you cannot overthrow it—lest you even be found to fight against God."

God doesn't need us to fight His battles, He is the One Who **fights for us**. It was Jesus Who said to love our enemies and pray for those who persecute you. He did not say to enter their worship services to interrupt them, nor to drown them in the river, nor to burn those damnable heretics at the stake.

God doesn't need us to fight His battles, He is the One Who fights for us.

When he, the Spirit of truth, is come, he will guide you into all truth: for he shall not speak of himself; but whatsoever he shall hear, that shall he speak: and he will show you things to come.- **John 16:13**

And as a final thought;

1 John 4:7-11

[7] Beloved, let us love one another, for love is of God; and everyone who loves is born of God and knows God. [8] He who does not love does not know God, for God is love. [9] In this the love of God was manifested toward us, that God has sent His only begotten Son into the world, that we might live through Him. [10] In this is love, not that we loved God, but that He loved us and sent His Son *to be* the propitiation for our sins. [11] Beloved, if God so loved us, we also ought to love one another.

AMEN.

About the author

REV. SAMUEL KADER is the author of the books:

OPENLY GAY, OPENLY CHRISTIAN, HOW THE BIBLE REALLY IS GAY FRIENDLY [1999, 2014, 2024] and

THE HOLY SPIRIT AND THE GAY COMMUNITY, THE EARLY YEARS. [2022]

Currently he pastors New Life Community Gospel Church in New Port Richey, Florida and is founder and president of S.K. Ministry Inc. He began actively pastoring in 1980, as the founding pastor of Reconciliation Metropolitan Community Church in Grand Rapids, Michigan. Since that time he has pastored 4 other churches, including the Community Gospel Church in Dayton, Ohio which he founded in 1986 and pastored for 30 years. For several years Pastor Kader's sermons reached out to the greater Dayton metropolitan area through a televised program called Eunique Perspectives of Hope which are now on YouTube (The Hope Tapes).

Pastor Kader has written several articles for both the gay press, and the gay Christian press, has appeared as a featured guest speaker at many regional and national conferences, and has traveled internationally. He held revivals for numerous churches and has spoken on many college campuses. Known for his thought-provoking insights and teachings, Reverend Kader delivers informative spiritual lessons with a sense of humor. With years of study and decades of pastoring experience he is uniquely qualified to report on the various moves of God up to and including the current move of God among the LGBT (+) community.

Samuel currently resides in Florida with his spouse Jerry, their dogs Duke, Dory, Dodi, and Dolly.

www.ingramcontent.com/pod-product-compliance
Lightning Source LLC
Chambersburg PA
CBHW051524120626
46551CB00012B/1067